HOW TO BE A GREAT MANAGER AND A GREAT LEADER BOTH AT THE WORK PLACE & AT HOME (Vols. 1-10)

2nd Edition

By Prince Gabriel

Hon. Member US Army, MBA, Doctorate in Management

JD Candidate, Boston, etc

Copyright Prince Gabriel 2011

Gabriel Atsepoyi
Honorable Member, US Army

All rights reserved. No part of this book may be reproduced or utilized in any form or by any means, electronic or mechanical, including photocopying, recording or by any information storage and retrieval systems, without the permission in writing from the publisher.

Library of Congress Cataloguing-in-Publication Data

ISBN 1463531907

Blue Sky Publisher, New York

Email: prince.gabriell@gmail.com. Phone 720 934 1983 USA

Copyright© 2011 by Gabriel B. Atsepoyi

ALL RIGHTS RESERVED

Manufactured in the United States of America

DEDICATION

This book is dedicated to all human beings, especially those who share the same belief with me: that education is forever. For that reason one should be in school and in the university or in the library reading and learning and learning and discovery something new and exciting always so that everyone can improve daily and help society have PEACE, better welfare for everyone and better productivity for society at large.

TABLE OF CONTENTS

1. Volume one: everyone is born to be a leader, but..., lessons of great leadership from the US Army, communication, great sex & leadership around page 5-44

2. Vol. two: have vision & telescope like Galilei, way forward, education, education, education around page 45-89

3. Vol. three: Ethics from childhood to be a great leader, the right quality education for our children, programs to keep kids safe from dangers around page 90-108

4. Vol. four: Traits of great leaders & specific things to do to be great managers/leaders, around page 109-141

5. Vol. five: learn to take care of infants to be great leader. Appeal to emotions (cry!), be proactive, speak the right language of the place, around page 142-159

6. Vol. six: understand your environment and comply with all relevant local laws, customs & usages. Most important learn and master all the ways to market your products & services for FREE! Using social networks & IT, p. 160-175

7. Vol. seven: carry your organization or nation across the Atlantic into the future. Make quality & safe things to sell overseas & buy less from overseas. No waste; recycle, re-use, reduce and save money for the future! Around page 176-2006

8. Vol. 8: Success from failures page 201-223

9. Vol. 9: How to prevent natural resources from drying up & things to invest in, like education, science page 224-276

10. Vol. 10: leaders earn your authority page 277-301

11. Anger Management & World Peace ideas added, pages 302 – 350

12. Epilogue: The building of a Nation or an Organization, using green initiatives and sustainable economic and/or business practices, pages 351-401

PREAMBLE

Without *PEACE,* nothing can be achieved productively. Without rational behavior or *Anger Management,* nothing can be achieved in any organization or nation. Green initiatives for sustainable economic and business practices, with innovative ideas, have been added to the epilogue. I have added these three books free of charge in this second edition for all managers and leaders reading this book.

Great managers, great leaders and great parenting skills, are qualities we all have from the day we were all born. Now, we all can choose to nurture our leadership skills, through education, skill training, through personal efforts by reading a lot of books, asking a lot of questions, and by employing the power of thinking, and thereby becoming more creative and innovative on a daily basis; or we can choose to keep our skills from birth. Either way everyone out there is capable of being a great manager, a great leader and a great parent, both at the work place and at home. The most important thing is to keep thinking: never stop thinking. Think. Think and innovate something new daily. Think creatively. Create something or lots of things in your lifetime that is unique only to you. Think of something good, write it down and publish it, build something, license it in your name, etc. Think.

Reach out and touch somebody's life at work or at school today. Shake somebody's hand today, somebody you have never met before. Ask that person how he/she is doing. Smile. Be genuine in your feelings of friendship. Be humane. Talk about your families, the good and the bad, to get that person to open up. Be natural. Such is the hallmark of a great leader. Practice it daily. Pass it on.

At the end of every day, evaluate everything you have done for the day and get independent people to also help you evaluate it to see what or how you could have done things better. Always do a follow-up and make corrections and take the necessary actions next time to do it better and improve significantly, alright.

Above all, keep putting oil in your lamp and keep it burning daily, and never, ever allow the oil in your lamp to dry out: just keep the lamp burning for as long as you live. That is what great managers do daily. That is what great leaders do daily. That is what great men and women, boys and girls are doing daily: improving their lives on a daily basis; getting better and better at school, at work, in colleges, and universities and in your behaviors and attitudes, etc. Yes, you can!

Unlike other traditional, boring leadership books out there, this book is very unique and innovative: there will be lots of funny stories and humor to drive the message home and make it stay with you forever. So, get ready to laugh!

INTRODUCTION/CHAPTER ONE

I know very little in life. The little I know I am going to be sharing with you here in part one of this paper, and several series to come in the future.

I served with Honors in the United States Army up till 2008. I studied Law from 1986 through 1990. I have a Degree in History from the University of Colorado, did the MBA twice, Masters in Project Management and have a Degree in the Executive MBA and currently doing my Doctorate in Management and a Candidate for the JD Degree in Law, Boston, etc.

Now, out of all my trainings and experiences in life, it is my experiences in the US Army that has influenced my leadership skills more than anything else. The United States Army taught me *LDRSHIP. L means leadership. D means duty. R means respect. S means Selfless service. H means honor. I, means integrity. P means personal courage.* This is very simple, right? This book is about management and leadership both at your home, and at your job. Charity, they say, begins at home, but must not stop there. Therefore, ideally you must be able to manage yourself (and your family) properly and productively before you can manage any organization or nation productively. The skills needed are both inborn and can be learned through on-the-job training and in regular academic classrooms. <u>Job training and retraining should be going on forever in order to remain competitive</u>, be #1 in your field, survive any turbulence or problems in the future and be forever productive and progressive. This is the premise of the book you are reading right now: leadership, duty, respect, selfless service, honor, integrity, and personal courage. Enjoy it!

CHAPTER TWO

THE LEADERSHIP STYLE OF WINSTON CHURCHILL

1. COMMUNICATION

Winston Churchill served in the British Army. Thereafter he became a politician always on the radio and TV warning the British people and the world about the danger posed by Adolf Hitler to the world. Nobody at the time took him serious until World War 11 (WW11) broke out in 1939. The British people got the message too late. To his credit Winston Churchill was made prime Minister during the war and helped to save the British people from extinction or total annihilation by the German bombardment.

2. During this turbulent time in WW11 there was never a day that went by that Winston Churchill did not called his wife or dropped her a note to tell her how much he loved her. Isn't that amazing? That is a true leader both at work and at home!

3. A great leader and a great manager today should and ought to use all areas of communications, the internet, twitter, emails, text message, telephones, and so on, to reach your lover or your spouse and your children, no matter how busy you might be. There is simply no excuse for failing the family or failing your co-workers. Reach out and touch somebody at work and at your home or family. Yes, you can! If Winston Churchill could do it while at war, yes, you too can do it!

4. If you must travel anywhere, take your spouse with you (<u>physically or in spirit</u>), even if you are going to war! Otherwise, there is simply no excuse for executives leaving their spouses behind and sleeping with prostitutes or having ex-marital affairs, eventually destroying their families, like Tiger Wood and Arnold Schwarzenegger did. You can manage both your work and family well and become a great leader like Winston Churchill. Yes, you can! Be smart. Use you intellect. Think. Think. Think!

5. GREAT SEX AND GREAT LEADERSHIP GO HAND-IN-HAND: In fact, after so many hectic board meetings and hard work, busy leaders and managers should be prepared to have great sex with their spouse or lover wherever they may be in the world (remember, always take your spouse or lover with you, <u>at least, in spirit</u>!), as illustrated below:

But first, please go and clean up! Take a clean shower, brush your teeth and clean your mouth and get every part of your body smelling naturally fresh and clean. Good!

Now, get some soft, nice music on, on a low volume and keep the light very dim.

Keep the temperature of the room very cool or very cold. Great sex flourishes well in cool or cold temperature.

STOP! Do not be in a rush. Take your time, caress...do it right!

The best way to do this is to illustrate this good art of lovemaking through the game of soccer. The man is going to play soccer with the woman or with his lover. It is going to be the game of competition.

Now the ball is set for the competition. The woman passes the ball to the man. The man meanders, heads the ball, tips one, tips two, and passes the ball back to the woman. The woman holds the ball, taps the ball on the head, toasts the ball in her tongue and the referee blows the whistle signaling a foul. The woman sets the ball back in her head, puts the ball between her inner thighs, the woman bounces the ball on her feet, rakes the ball up to her chest, the woman shoulders the ball, the woman places the ball in her ear lobes, then the ball rolls down to her neck through her shoulders and the ball gets stuck in the woman's inner thighs. Finally, the woman gets the ball out, kisses the ball and passes the ball to the man, the man toast the ball, twist the ball in his hand, does a back slide and runs with the ball to the center court. The man tips one, tips two, tips three, tips four, tips five, the man changes position, travels back north and did the a back slide toast the ball in the air and presses harder towards the goalie. The man meanders, shoulders the ball, sweating profusely and the crowd is shouting "Go man! Go man!" and the man pushing towards the goalie pressing harder, leans forward tips one, two , three, four, sets the ball and shoots. Ladies and Gentlemen "It's a GOAL! Goal!! Goal!!! Gooooaaaaallllllllllllll!!!!

Great job!

1. As you can see here great sex is not a selfish act or art. Great sex does not operate in a vacuum. Great sex is not for unproductive, idle people; rather, great sex ought to be for great people doing great things to move society forward, alright.

2. One *caveat* here: if you must have great sex with unknown, multiple partners or strangers, please protect yourself by wearing good condoms. Remember: one wife or girlfriend, one trouble, two wives or two girlfriends, two troubles, three lovers, three troubles...so how many troubles do you want in your life?

3. Ha. Ha. Ha.

Well, below is the result of not being faithful to your lover:

The Cowboy who lost his wife

The sea will be empty where there is no boat to come. The road will go on forever when the horse does not pass along it. The moons will have no significance when there is no reason to count them.

But, one is always sad to lose the moon and sun. It is only possible to look from afar but that does not make the day and night any less black when they have gone.

John Johnston was born in 1909 in Wyoming. He was a young cowboy truly in love with his High School sweetheart, Susan, in the 20s. John was very handsome, gentle, and respectful of women as a young man. John was also a devoted man who never missed weekend service every time. John's father, Dr. Pepper, was an aristocrat, who used to owe his own private hospital, called Dr. Pepper's Infirmary. Dr. Pepper also owned a farm and several John Deere equipments to plow and work on the farmland.

In 1926, John's father passed away at the age of 60. The following year, 1927, John's mother also passed away. John, now an orphan, graduated from High School in 1928. The same year he proposed and married Susan, his High School sweetheart. In 1929 John and Susan gave birth to a son whom they named Jake. Right after the birth of their son the Stock Exchange crashed sending the United States economy into the worse depression in US history that lasted from 1929 till 1939. Consequently, John lost his job as a bank clerk. With no money and no food in the house life became very unbearable for the young couple. After about six months of hunger and starvation, John could not take the heat any longer and so he turned to alcohol; eventually he got hooked to alcohol and women. Susan, on the other hand was a nice, righteous, honest woman who believes in integrity, family, community and God.

With no money and food, John started stealing from other people, gambles his loots away only to steal more again. He frequented beer parlors and spends his time with younger girls and the outlaws. Susan on the other hand held on strongly to her virtues, manages to clean people's homes for a dollar or two with which to buy a loaf of bread for Jake to survive the day while John wasted away.

Sometimes John would come home very late at night, after many days outside, heavily drunk, and with his keys lost or forgotten inside the bras of other girls, would pound on the door with rage: "open the door, Sus!" John would scream at the top of his voice.

"Who is it?" Susan would demand to know, as the voice of her husband had grown unfamiliar while heavily intoxicated by the day.

"Johnny! It's your Johnny, babie!"

After hesitating for a while Susan would usually open the door for John to come in. But after three years of the same life Susan decided not to open the door at night for John. That is when John turned violent as John would forcibly open the door at night and out of frustration would beat Susan all night while Jake curled under the dining table scared to death.

This physical abuse went on for a while until Jake turned nine and Susan became weary and sick of John's abuse. Jake too now felt remorse and detached from a father he never had. Sex between John and Susan was a thing of the past as John now satisfies himself with younger girls on the streets while leaving Susan and Jake to fend for themselves. To add insult to injury, one night John actually had the audacity, the temerity and the effrontery to bring one of his girls home not only to pass the night but to have sex with her in their bedroom while Susan and Jake slept in the living room! That was the last straw for Susan! At this point on all the feelings Susan ever had for John vanished for good. For Susan henceforth it was time to move on; and move on she did.

Susan was only twenty eight years old, still very pretty, hot and available. She had gone without love and sex for nine years; nine whole years! "I wonder how many women out there could stay with this type of physical abuse, dishonesty and no sex for nine whole years!" Susan thought to herself.

Seeing to it the John was no longer interested in her Susan decided enough was enough and that she must move on in life. But John was her first man and Susan had never allowed other guys to come close to her before. First, Susan had to learn quickly from the younger girls how to be sexy again by wearing transparent clothes to show her beautiful skin. She needed some make-ups, nice shoes, perfumes and all the things she never had to make herself look gorgeous and to attract young guys.

Susan needed a friend or some girl friends so bad. So the following weekend instead of joining the company of married couples as she had done for the past nine years, this particular weekend Susan decided to join the singles or unmarried people in the weekend school class. The young girls were very excited to meet Susan. At the end of the class Susan befriended a young beautiful girl named Toni, who was turning 26 years that day, and she too was desperate for a man. During the weekend school class Susan hid her wedding ring at home and announced to everyone that she was single and available. On Toni's birthday, Toni arranged for a birthday bash at her apartment that night and invited two of the most handsome singles in the weekend class besides Susan and herself for all night party. Susan quickly arranged for a baby-sitter for the night and made her-self beautiful and attractive for the birthday party at Toni's place.

On arrival at Toni's place two handsome guys were at the table. One introduced himself to be Peter, sitting very close to Toni indicating that an accord had been struck between Peter and Toni. While the other guy, Charles, a tall, slim, very handsome school teacher from the suburb introduced himself to Susan: "hello Susan, my name is Charles, how are you?" "I'm fine", Susan managed a smile, but still very shy.

Without much ado Toni proposed a toast to everyone and called for the party to begin. There was plenty to eat and drink.

In fact, every jar in Toni's apartment was filled with various pop drinks and mixed with alcohol of all sorts, from brandy to whiskey, wine and beer. There was no water to be had for the night. It was a suicide mission. Toni had planned the night for everyone to get drunk and get hooked up and for good sex she had been craving for, for a very long time.

However, both Charles and Peter were good gentlemen who were not used to alcohol and promiscuous sex, especially with strangers. So, at first they were very shy, taking their time to show the best behavior and respect for the ladies. But after three hours of soaking alcohol in their bodies, decency and respectability gave way to ecstasy, gyration, singing, dancing, laughing, kissing and of course the greatest sex of their lives! It was sex galore as each party settles down for a good night of sexual rendezvous. It was a night unlike any in the lives of two women with two strange guys from a weekend class.

For the first time in nine years Susan was able again to feel the surge, the heat and the rush of a man inside her as <u>Charles took his time all night long to caress, kiss and show true romance and respect to Susan; making sweet love to Susan; giving her a slow and gentle thrusting and **holding himself back for one to two hours**, allowing Susan to climax first</u> before finally coming with a gush which can be liken to the force of an avalanche!

When the night was over it was the dawn of a new day for both Susan and Toni. At last both women finally found good, honest men who also <u>knew everything about romance, **respect** and how to take good care of the woman.</u>

It didn't take long for John Johnston to notice the change in Susan's life as she sings and smiles every time without any notice of John around her. Susan practically stops any kind of conversation with John and spends most of the days and nights away at Charles's apartment while leaving Jake for John to baby-sit. It was an agonizing moment for John. After six months John could not take it anymore. John, the cowboy, now realized he had lost his High School queen for good. Susan was gone to the point of no return.

So, John, the cowboy, went to a lawyer to get a divorce to officially end the marriage between him and Susan. On arrival at the lawyer's office to seek a divorce the following conversations ensued:

"Do you have any grounds?" the lawyer asks.

"Yep, I got about a hunnered acres" the proud cowboy beams.

"No, you don't understand", the lawyer says.

"Do you have a case?"

"Nope, I ain't got a Case, but I got a John Deere".

"I mean do you have a grudge?"

"Yep, it's where I park my John Deere"

"No, sir, I mean do you have a suit?"

"Yep, I wear it to work every day"

"Well, sir, does your wife beat you up?"

"Nope, we both git up about 4:30"

The exasperated lawyer tries another tack.

"Let me put it this way: why do you want a divorce?"

The cowboy shuffles his muddy boots, "Well, I can't have a meaningful conversation with her".

As anyone can see from this story, our knowledge and understanding of girls and women are still in the dark wood. If we cannot yet detect with certainty the first rays of a rosy dawn, neither can there yet be felt the first rumblings of the earthquake of disaster. So, be smart. Be rational. Be fair.

Take care of your lover/spouse always. Buy her/him nice things. Buy her/him flowers. Show concern. Be helpful. Be considerate. Be there always to help in any form or shape. Be reasonable. Do the right thing for her/him. Be thankful daily. <u>Be good. Be good. Be good.</u> Take proper care of your lover/spouse or else…

Take good care of yourself, eat balanced diet, lots of fruits and vegetables, and drink water daily, exercise daily, please fall in love have good sex more frequently, keep good friends who are ready to be educated and work hard in life to enjoy their lives, be friendly with everyone regardless of race, gender, ethnicity, greed or religion, make everyone your friend and your family, give to the poor always, help the needy always, be the first to say hello to friends and strangers, be smart and stay away from trouble always, talk less, listen more, better yourself daily, improve your life daily, forgive always, respect and protect girls and women always, laugh daily and be around happy people, do humor, take life easy, enjoy life while it lasts, go out and get the millions of dollars waiting for you, since no one is born to be poor, get education and seek information daily, be rich in morality, do those things that are excellent, and have lots, and lots of fun! Bye!

This is Gabriel Atsepoyi, an American Soldier. He studied Law (LL.B), BA History, MBA and a Doctorate Degrees in Management. (Univ of Colorado, Cambridge, Boston JD, etc). **If you have special talent and you want sponsorship to the USA or any country, please get in touch with me pronto**. You can also consult me for Leadership ideas, and ways to improve any government or corporation. I **am ready and able to help the USA Government or Nigeria Government anytime. Please call me! 720 934 1983 USA.**

CONTACT ME ANYTIME: prince.gabriell@gmail.com or atsepoyi@hotmail.com

Telephone number in the United States: 720 934 1983

Or write to me regarding any other business you wish to do with me, like Wealth Management, Partnerships, or any issue, etc. Send your letters to:

Gabriel B. Atsepoyi

Doctorate program

5775 DTC BLVD, SUITE 100

GREENWOOD VILLAGE, COLORADO 80111 USA

FAX 303 694 6673

THE BOOK OF TOTAL HAPPINESS
by Gabriel B. Atsepoyi (Akpieyi)

Education is the key to learning any subject better, so why should it be any different when it comes to being happy? This is the premise for Gabriel Atsepoyi's *The Book of Total Happiness*, in which the author gives new meaning to the search for happiness and contentment in one's life.

It has been said that psychological maturity is achieved when one gains a secure understanding of the meaning of life and one's place in it. This fascinating volume explores this matter in full detail concerning happiness, marriage, health and physical well being.

Regardless of religious or philosophical persuasion, readers will become engrossed in this presentation, which to its credit does not intend to talk down to readers, but instead provides working guidelines in a straightforward and easily understood fashion.

Given the high rate of divorce these days, Mr. Atsepoyi believes that without some form of education concerning marriage, the do's and don'ts, the expectations and the compromises, people are destined to continue to allow this shocking statistic to grow. This book's goal, therefore, is to begin that education, to provide understandable paths toward that elusive spiritual habitat, being happy. It's not as easy as it seems, says the author, and most people have to work at it. Yet, it is not totally out of reach, if one can look at life with honest appraisal and work to change those things that hinder one's happiness.

One of the more intriguing aspects of this book is the point that not everyone achieves the same level of happiness, nor has the same avenues available to them in their search for personal happiness. That is fine, says the author, because no two people are exactly the same. Each must find that place that is comfortable for him or her, then work to maintain those good feelings through effort and commitment.

Mr. Atsepoyi's prose is fluid and expressive, and his observations are shrewdly punctuated by a basic wisdom that will appeal to all. But what makes this book be singled out from the many is the significant contribution it makes toward re-educating people of the how and why of being happy. This serves a most practical purpose, first in helping the reader to find paths and guidelines for being happy, the author is also boldly illustrating the power of individual expression, positive thinking, and having a goal to work toward.

Highly recommended for its insight and analyses, *The Book of Total Happiness*, by Gabriel Atsepoyi, is must reading. The author's ideas are lucid and innovative, portraying much wisdom and common sense, and combining all these attributes into one volume enables each reader to further his or her education on perhaps the most important subject matter existing today, the art of being happy.

Section Two of the book focuses on: A-Z about HIV/AIDS and the latest facts on AIDS, protection for kids and family, women's rights (the need to respect and protect women), smoking and its hazards, environmental protection/prevention, how and the need for better education for children, etc., etc.

THE BOOK OF TOTAL HAPPINESS

ABOUT THE AUTHOR

Gabriel Atsepoyi (Akpieyi), twenty-six years old, was born in Africa and presently resides in Colorado.

An avid reader, Mr. Atsepoyi makes it known that the only way he is happy is when he is helping others. His love of God serves his existence well, as he expands upon his belief that one's knowledge is one's power in leading a happy and successful life.

A member of the Optimist Club of Arvada, the author has had many articles published previously on a variety of topics, yet his overriding concerns are for the rate of divorce and its effects toward broken homes, unhappy families, neglected children, uneducated and uncultured children, and crime. He has propounded many solutions in these areas in his latest work, and his hope is that readers will reflect upon those suggestions.

THE BOOK OF TOTAL HAPPINESS

by Gabriel B. Atsepoyi (Akpieyi)

Education is the key to learning any subject better, so why should it be any different when it comes to being happy? This is the premise for Gabriel Atsepoyi's *The Book of Total Happiness*, in which the author gives new meaning to the search for happiness and contentment in one's life.

It has been said that psychological maturity is achieved when one gains a secure understanding of the meaning of life and one's place in it. This fascinating volume explores this matter in full detail concerning happiness, marriage, health and physical well-being. Regardless of religious or philosophical persuasion, readers will become engrossed in this presentation, which to its credit does not intend to talk down to readers, but instead provides working guidelines in a straightforward and easily understood fashion.

Given the high rate of divorce these days, Mr. Atsepoyi believes that without some form of education concerning marriage the do's and don't's, the expectations and the compromises, people are destined to continue to allow this shocking statistic to grow. This book's goal, therefore, is to begin that education, to provide understandable paths toward that elusive spiritual habitat, being happy. It's not as easy as it seems, says the author, and most people have to work at it. If it is not totally out of reach, if one can look at life with honest appraisal and work to change those things that hinder one's happiness.

One of the more intriguing aspects of the book is the point that not everyone achieves the same level of happiness, nor has the same avenues available to them in their search for personal happiness. That is fine, says the author, because no two people are exactly the same. Each must fine that place that is comfortable for him or her, then work to maintain those good feelings through effort and commitment.

Mr. Atsepoyi's prose is fluid and expressive, and his observations are shrewdly punctuated by a basic wisdom that will appeal to all. But what makes this book be singled out from the many is the significant contribution it makes toward re-educating people of the how and why of being happy. This serves a most practical purpose, first in helping the reader to find paths and guidelines for being happy, the author is also boldly illustrating the power of individual expression, positive thinking, and having a goal to work toward.

Highly recommended for its insight and analyses, *The Book of Total Happiness*, by Gabriel Atsepoyi, is must reading. The author's ideas are lucid and innovative, portraying much wisdom and common sense, and combining all these attributes into one volume enables each reader to further his or her education on perhaps the most important subject matter existing today, the art of being happy.

Section Two of the book focuses on: A-Z about HIV/AIDS and the latest facts on AIDS, protection for kids and family, women's rights (the need to respect and protect women), smoking and its hazards, environmental protection/prevention, how and the need for better education for children, etc., etc.

THE BOOK OF TOTAL HAPPINESS

ABOUT THE AUTHOR

Gabriel Atsepoyi (Akpieyi), twenty-six years old, was born in Africa and presently resides in Colorado.

An avid reader, Mr. Atsepoyi makes it known that the only way he is happy is when he is helping others. His love of God serves his existence well, and expands upon his belief that one's knowledge gets one's power in leading a happy and successful life.

A member of the Optimist Club of Arvada, the author has had many articles published previously on a variety of topics, yet his overriding concerns are for the rate of divorce and its effects toward broken homes, unhappy families, neglected children, uneducated and uncultured children, and crime. He has propounded many solutions in these areas in his latest work, and his hope is that readers will reflect upon those suggestions.

ISBN 0-9634951-0-X

9 780963 695109

HOW TO BE A GREAT LEADER AND A GREAT MANAGER BOTH AT THE WORK PLACE & AT HOME (PART 2)

PART TWO (NOTE: SO MANY SERIES COMING IN THE FUTURE)

By Prince Gabriel

Hon. Member US Army, MBA, Doctorate in Management

JD Candidate

Copyright © Prince Gabriel 2011

PREAMBLE

Can you make jokes? Can you create humors? Can you <u>learn how to make people laugh</u> to sell your vision?

Do you have a vision like Google or China? Do you have a vision for your organization or nation? Do you have a vision for your life or family? Do you have a mission for your organization or nation? Do you have a mission for your life or family? Do you have some objectives or plans or strategies mapped out on how to achieve your vision and mission?

Galileo Galilei (1564-1642) looked into the sky with his telescope and saw the moon and the stars, the preamble to the scientific revolution we have today. Can you look into the sky and come out with your own revolution? Do you have a telescope to look into the future? Can you look several years ahead and think what might be and take the necessary actions to get there before others? In the tumultuous road ahead to the future, can you compete with others in a global village and gain a competitive edge to be number one, and remain number one in the future?

Can you give hopes to people? Can you help make those hopes real? <u>Can you help to actualize hopes for humans? Can you?</u>

Do you have what it takes to <u>earn everyone's trust</u> to cooperate with you and/or compromise with everyone in order to move forward productively?

Can you get everyone on board with you and move your organization or nation forward, <u>prudently, at the speed of light,</u> in the competition for future market shares?

Do you have enough academic training and on the job training or experiences like Jack Welch of General Electric or like Margaret Thatcher of Great Britain to get your organization or nation to the future without falling asleep on the wheel, crashing and killing everyone on board? Do you? Can you honestly state this fact in black and white, in your own handwriting, and sign it in the presence of a Notary Public, for future reference? Please ponder over these questions in part two of this book. Again, as I wrote above and below:

Great managers, great leaders and great parenting skills, are qualities we all have from the day we were all born. Now, we all can choose to nurture our leadership skills, through education, skill training, through personal efforts by reading a lot of books, asking a lot of questions, and by employing the power of thinking, and thereby becoming more creative and innovative on a daily basis; or we can choose to keep our skills from birth. Either way everyone out there is capable of being a great manager, a great leader and a great parent, both at the work place and at home. The most important thing is to keep thinking: never stop thinking. Think. Think and innovate something new daily. Think creatively. Create something or lots of things in your lifetime that is unique only to you. Think of something good, write it down and publish it, build something, license it in your name, etc. Think.

Reach out and touch somebody's life at work or at school today. Shake somebody's hand today, somebody you have never met before. Ask that person how he/she is doing. Smile. Be genuine in your feelings of friendship. Be humane. Talk about your families, the good and the bad, to get that person to open up. Be natural. Such is the hallmark of a great leader. Practice it daily. Pass it on.

At the end of every day, evaluate everything you have done for the day and get independent people to also help you evaluate it to see what or how you could have done things better. Always do a follow-up and make corrections and take the necessary actions next time to do it better and improve significantly, alright.

Above all, keep putting oil in your lamp and keep it burning daily, and never, ever allow the oil in your lamp to dry out: just keep the lamp burning for as long as you live. That is what great managers do daily. That is what great leaders do daily. That is what great men and women, boys and girls are doing daily: improving their lives on a daily basis; getting better and better at school, at work, in colleges, and universities and in your behaviors and attitudes, etc. Yes, you can!

CHAPTER ONE

HAVE A VISION & A TELESCOPE LIKE GALILEO GALILEI

If you want to be great or be number one in the future, you can follow the footsteps of great men and women out there; or follow the footsteps of great nation, if you are a developing country trying to develop and be like the industrialized nations. You can copy everything the great organizations like Google and Microsoft are doing, perfect it, and perhaps be like the great ones. You can hire the smartest and most intelligent people from the best universities in the world, like Google and Microsoft or the Obama White House, are doing, copy everything, and modify everything to fit into your setting. That is one of the easiest ways to be number one and be great.

However, if you want to live a memory mark on earth, and change human course for the better, to make a turnaround in people's lives for the best, then, please be like Galileo Galilei! Or be like Charles Darwin! Or be like Nelson Mandela! Or be like Mother Teresa! Or be like Mahatma Gandhi! These are all visionary people that have left indelible marks in our lives.

Now, what is your vision for your organization or nation again?

THE WAY FORWARD: EDUCATION, EDUCATION, EDUCATION

No nation or organization can succeed and be number one, and remain number one, if its entire workforce is not properly educated like Google and Microsoft employees are. By education here, I mean the kind of quality education in Japan, Germany, United Kingdom, United States ivory league schools, and China, and so on. **Please train your workers/people daily**.

Educating the people in your country or organization should be an on-going process. Organizations and nations should please make it mandatory for its workforce and its people to be taking some university courses on how to improve operations, themselves and customer services regularly, forever. Education is forever! Without it, please do not retain employment of your staff! Everyone coming onboard should be ready for daily training. That is the way forward. Please explain this fact well.

THINGS TO DO TO EARN THE TRUST OF OTHERS

1. Make eye contact, be the first to say hello
2. Shake hands, touch people in a friendly way
3. Get together after work; be interested in each other's best meal or cultures, etc. Socialize during and after work.
4. Learn each other's language and make a genuine effort to speak it continuously
5. Get to know each other's problems, lend a helping hand
6. Have dinner or lunch together more frequently and get the kids to bond with each other or possibly get marry when they grow up. One of the secrets in life is that no nation or

family friendship with other families ever ceases to exist where the kids have some strong bonds together, and kids are encouraged to solidify the bond of friendship forever! For instance, the mistrust and quagmire between some Afghanistan rulers and some Americans, or between some Pakistanis and some Americans, or between the rulers of Iran, North Koreans and the Americans can be ended for good with children of these countries getting to know themselves early enough in friendship, love bonds and everlasting bonds through marriages! I hope somebody is listening!

7. You can establish bond and trust by getting people to eat with their hands from the same plate with you to foster human-touch and camaraderie. It is almost impossible for your friend or co-worker eating from the same plate to

betray you or not help you out in times of trouble or danger.

8. Take a shower together. Get to see each other's nakedness. That is another secret. Ideally, same-sex employee, in a none sexual mode can familiarize self and get to that comfortable, last stage of bonding, by taking showers together, and discussing freely, past exploits with girls or guys. That was exactly what Winston Churchill did during World War Two when he arrived at the White House in Washington DC to beg Franklin D Roosevelt for ammunitions to stop the German onslaught on the British people. In order to gain the trust of President Roosevelt for a secret Lease of war munitions, which was probably illegal, but doable at the time, Winston Churchill, the then

Prime Minister of Great Britain, took off all his clothes and became naked before President Roosevelt, and it worked!

9. Practice human-touch, without breaking the law, on sexual harassment. Ask if it is ok to touch or praise somebody or your co-worker. Say something nice always. Comfort somebody in a sorrowful mode. Go out of your way, if you can, and buy somebody some gifts without asking or accepting anything back in return. It is called human-touch. Practice it daily. Gain people's trust. Please be transparent or open with everything; and let there be no hidden agenda. Remember, you might have some enemies, plotting against you all the time. So, please, please, please, be honest, and be open, and let other people know that your intentions are good. Integrity, ok.

10. Be fair. Show fairness. Practice justice and fairness in every dealing with people. Be honest. Let people see it without you trying to convince people about you. Be natural. Be bonding and let trust flow naturally.

Take the necessary ACTIONS and practice everything here to earn the trust of people in your organization or nation, for your progress and better productivity.

11. Please be open or transparent. Communicate clearly both orally and in writing. Communicate. Communicate. Learn and master the act or art of communication in person, via twitter or the internet, by emails, face book, by writing something, like a note or letter, with your handwriting. Yes, your handwriting, and not typing it. **Leaders please write with your handwriting to praise people more frequently. People appreciate that a lot!**

Trust me here; besides other modern ways of communications. Communicate with your friends, co-worker, families and your people; just practice effective communication, period!

12. Please make people happy! Happy people are productive people! That fact is indisputable ok. Whether you are the manager or leader of an organization or the President of a country, please, please, please, figure out how to get your people to be happy naturally. Figure out how to get everyone to have quality education and possess great skills to make themselves happy about their worth in life. It is true you cannot satisfy everyone, but you, as a leader MUST try to do just that! Please try to make people happy. Train people to have solid skills that are marketable anywhere in the world; that is one of the

best ways to make everyone happy! <u>Request the very best in quality</u> and quantity contribution from everyone, like the teachers and scientists, the police men and women, the Soldiers of your country; and for goodness sake <u>increase the salaries of these great men and women!</u>

13. HUMOR: learn it and give at least one joke daily, both at work and at home. Telling good jokes is perhaps one of the very best ways to sell your vision, earn everyone's trust, bond with people and get everyone on board. It is extremely effective, trust me here. Please practice it daily and become an expert in telling jokes and humors. Get people to laugh daily to ease tensions and to fall in love with you. Please give the same amount of love back to others. Be realistic. Be pragmatic. Be futuristic.

14. If you must use surveillance camera or other IT gadgets to monitor your people progress or other activities, as is the case with most organizations and nations today, for goodness please be open, transparent and be kind and honest enough to let everyone know about it and give clear reasons for everyone to sign on to it. Never hide and do stuffs like that if you want everyone to trust you and be on board with you. Please be fair.

15. Play soccer, football, rackets, baseballs and other games together more frequently for camaraderie or bonding. Please make jokes daily. Do fun stuffs together. Encourage jokes, have competitions for the best, clean humors or jokes and reward people well for good humor. Good luck!

Below is a funny story for you. Enjoy it!

On January 23, 1995, I met with an agent of the Federal Bureau of Investigation (FBI, that is the <u>old FBI</u>. The <u>new FBI is very efficient and productive</u>) in Denver, Colorado. The name of the agent is Charles R. Kasson. My mission to the FBI was to complain about fraud and how one Mr. William Lake in Washington D.C. defrauded my oldest brother, Murphy, of $120,000. The events and conversations you are about to read are true and very, very funny. Are you ready? Here we go:

Gabriel: My name is Gabriel. I came here today to complain about a fraud and/or what happened about four and half years ago.

FBI Agent: Why did you wait this long to report this?

Gabriel: Because I couldn't locate his address. The Better Business Bureau (BBB) in Washington D. C. helped me to locate the address last December.

FBI Agent: Well, I have been doing this job for about or a little bit more than 30 years and I retire in 11 months. I am going to try to play double advocate. How did this fraud occur and where?

Gabriel: Well, Mr. William Lake told my brother, Murphy, that he could ship tons of frozen fish to West Africa provided he, Murphy, gives him $120,000 to represent 50% of the freight amount. Murphy is the Managing Director of his company (MACON LTD) while I was the legal officer. At the time of the transaction I was already residing in the United States. So Mr. Lake collected $120,000 and never delivered anything of value in return. The contract for the supply of fish was either frustrated and/or cancelled because the fish he, Mr. Lake, wanted to export to West Africa from Chile/Peru was contaminated according to reports in various media globally.

So the fish he was trying to export to Africa was not good for consumption according to the Governments of Chile and Peru. Hitherto he has refused to refund the $120,000 he collected I am very unhappy about his activities and I want you the FBI people to get him criminally.

FBI Agent: Well, this guy may be a good guy. May be something went wrong during the negotiation and may be he already spent the $120,000 to pay his bills and overhead cost. May be he is a crook. You see, we have loads of cases like this and sometimes we put them aside to handle those that involve millions and billions of dollars in scam. Your case may not be looked at for months or years but I am going to log it in anyway.

You see, you are from Nigeria, and most of the Nigerians in the United States are crooks. That is not to say that you are one of them, but, eh, that is how the system is...May be the agent who is going to work on your case is on vacation and when he/she gets back he/she hasn't received his/her pay check from the government. May be his/her work load is too much to handle this kind of case. May be, anything, just may be, you know. I don't know...

Gabriel: Sir, I came here because my company was defrauded of $120,000. Can you help me please!

FBI Agent: Perhaps I am going to take a look at your complaint later but not right now. Some of us just work for free these days. May be Murphy himself should come to the U. S. and tell me all the stories. May be it's just a civil matter with a little bit of criminal activities attached to it.

Gabriel: Sir, if I took somebody's $120,000 four years ago in America I would be in jail by now. Can you help me please!!!

FBI Agent: You see, I don't know this guy called William Lake. The FBI is not here to ruin people's business. Where was the money paid from anyway?

Gabriel: From our London accounts.

FBI Agent: So your company is in London? You see we have problems here. We have inherent problems.

Gabriel: Our company, MACON LTD, has its headquarters in London and Nigeria and I am the agent in the United States.

FBI Agent: Oh, I see. So, the money was wired to Mr. Lake from London to Washington D. C.

Gabriel: Yes.

FBI Agent: Thru what bank and what is the account number?

Gabriel: I don't know. But I can get them for you.

FBI Agent: You see Mr...is it ok to just call you Gabriel?

Gabriel: Yeah.

FBI Agent: You see Gabriel, I am going to log the complaint in may be today or tomorrow or next...The complaint would then go to the 8th floor. From there to the 1st floor. From there to the 17th floor...Then somebody would have to proofread it at the 4th floor. From there to the 3rd floor. From there to the 17th floor. From there may be back to the 17th floor or 18th floor. From there to the 11th or 12th floor. From there may be back to the 1st or 2rd or 3rd floor. From there to the 18th or 17th or 16th or 15th or 14th or 13th or 12th or 11th or 10th or 9th floor...from there may be finally to Washington D. C. and *whatever happens in Washington D. C. , you see I don't know. In fact, I don't like Washington D. C. I haven't been to D. C. and I don't want to go there. So if this report (that's if) it gets to Washington D. C. only God knows what they are going to do with it there. I don't know Gabriel...*

Gabriel: Is this the FBI office?!

FBI Agent: Yes it is! I am just telling you how the system works. You see, may be the Government is going to close tomorrow. May be if I log this complaint now I probably wouldn't be able to look at it for days or months. May be this time that I am spending with you my desk in the office is getting piles and piles of complaints. May be this guy Mr. Lake has been good once and a crook 99%. If that is so then we have problems bringing such a person to prosecution. The FBI is not going to knock on Mr. Lake's door tomorrow. The FBI is not going to get people out of business. I am only going to do the best I can until I retire in about 11 months or so. May be the Government is going to shut down soon again. You see Gabriel I...I...don't like Washinton DC. I...I..don't know how long this is going to take. I am just telling you the facts: Washington DC stinks...

Gabriel: Sir, Mr. Lake collected $120,000 and gave back nothing of value in return. Do you understand that?

FBI Agent: You see Gabriel, I know you're a law officer in your country, but I am only an accountant, working as a special agent with the FBI. I have been doing this work for about 30 years. I know what you're talking about. I am going to write the report today. May be today or tomorrow or next week. I shall ask my secretary to proofread it or I shall proofread it myself. May be I can do that in the evening…You see I am going to retire in about 11 months…I am 55years and I have been doing this job for more than 30 years! Ok, this is what I am going to do. I am going to call the BBB in Washington DC and ask for more details ok Gabriel.

Gabriel: I called Mr. Lake on the phone this morning. For the first time in two months he answered the phone. I discovered he has an accent. It appears to me he is not one of the regular guys here; I mean he doesn't have your accent and doesn't speak like somebody who was born here.

FBI Agent: Is that right?!

Gabriel: Oh yes!

FBI Agent: Well then, I am going to check this William Lake out immediately then. But remember the FBI is not in the business of driving people out of business ok. I don't know when I would be able to do anything about your complaint. I don't know anything about Washington DC. I cannot do anything to William Lake in Denver. By law the criminal action can only commence in Washington DC. I don't like Washington DC. All I can do is submit the report to Washington DC. That is all I can do. I don't know what is going to happen from there on. May be the guy in Washington DC is on vacation. May be he/she is about to go on vacation. May be he/she is just coming back from vacation. May be his/her desk is already full with complaints/assignments. May be the government will shut down as soon as the report gets to Washington DC…Just may be..You see Gabriel I …I..don't know what's going to happen.

Gabriel: Is there anyway you can give me a note to Mr. Lake to refund the $120,000 quietly without having to go thru the government's red tape as you told me?

FBI Agent: Oh no! You see, at the FBI we don't and cannot give you or write anything for you on our letter head. Everything about the FBI is done in secret. I can't even tell you that I am writing a report on this man called William Lake. If the press should call now they are not going to get anything from us. We at the FBI don't tell anybody anything we do or anything we are doing. If you call on the phone to inquire about anything or anybody all you are going to get from us is "no comment". That is it. We only pass our information thru a very tight channel: from the 17th floor thru the 2nd floor to the 18th floor and back to the 1st, 2nd, 5th, 3rd, 18th, 16th and back to the 3rd, to the 11th and to the 12th, 13th and 14th floor; and back to the 8th, 7th floor…and thence finally to Washington DC, and whatever happens in Washington DC is none of my business. I don't know. I don't even want to know ok.

Gabriel (sighing): So, how can I get back the $120,000 collected by Mr. Lake for which nothing of value was given in return?

FBI Agent: May be Mr. Lake used part of the money and may be he already used all of the money to pay overhead costs or to pay his debt or something. May be he didn't know the transaction wouldn't be consummated but used the money anyway. Or may be too many businesses pulled out or called off *business deals with him after he may have paid for people making arrangements to commence the transactions. Or may be this guy is simply a crook. You see a lot of the information you have given to me so far sounds like a civil matter to me. You see Gabriel if that is the case the FBI is not in the business of money collecting. You probably need to file a civil case in the court, if you haven't done so. In your case we have to be able to establish fraud before we can even start to do anything about your case. In fact, the FBI may not even look at your case at all considering the amount involved – only $120,000! The last time a complaint of about $100,000 was brought to my desk I never touched it.*

Gabriel: Why?

FBI Agent: Because there are more pressing things to do. Like those involving millions and billions of dollars in thefts and fraudulent activities. Those are the complaints that attract our attention. Those are the cases that we are more likely to work on; not a mere $120,000! In your case I don't even know what's going to happen. May be nobody is even going to touch it.

Gabriel: I hear the statute of limitation is about 5 years for criminal matter. Can you do something before the time runs out?

FBI Agent: I can't promise or assure you that anything would be done at anytime. Even if I decide to handle your case right now at this hour of 10am, and get all the machinery in motion: from me to my secretary, to the undersecretary to my supervisor to the lower level supervisor to the proofreading stage, to gathering all the evidences to doing all the investigations to correcting mistakes to requesting for more information, to when my next vacation is due, up to the time of my return from my vacation, to the time when all the facts are typed out, up to when everything is given to the mail man, to when the mail man finishes with the packaging, to when the mail man gets thru downtown Denver, to when he stops for his lunch, to when he heads to the post office, to when he gets thru the long line at the post office, to when he finally gets to the postmaster, to when the postmaster is able to fly to Washington DC because of the blizzards or other inconveniences there, to when the mail finally gets to Washington DC's office…gosh, this stage of getting things to Washington DC alone can take about or at the least one year. So as you can see we have inherent problems.

Gabriel: I think am going to fly to Washington DC to start everything there next week.

FBI Agent: Look Gabriel I can't guarantee you that all the paper work will be ready in Washington DC when you get there next week. In fact, by next week your complaint might still be below thousands of others on my desk. So don't count on that ok. I can't even start writing the report now until I get all the information from you or from Murphy. May be you can tell Murphy to send all the documents to me by the fastest mail available instead of faxing it. Do you have United States Consular in Nigeria?

Gabriel: Yes we do.

FBI Agent: I didn't know that. Where is Nigeria anyway?

Gabriel: Nigeria is situated in West Africa.

FBI Agent: you said your business is in London and where in Nigeria?

Gabriel: Lagos, Nigeria.

FBI Agent: Never heard of Lagos before.

Gabriel: Lagos was the capital of Nigeria. It is still the commercial capital, while Abuja is now the current capital of Nigeria. But sir I am here to talk about getting the refund of $120,000 from Mr. William Lake. What can you do as an FBI agent to ensure the possibility of getting the $120,000 back from Mr. Lake?

FBI Agent: I am just going to write the report whenever and send it out whenever and wait. May be the government is going to close down today or tomorrow, I don't know. There are certain things beyond our control. It is not that I am trying not to help you. I just can't chew more than I can bite. The FBI is presently saturated with work. This is compounded by the fact that we may be working for free without pay for weeks or months to come, especially if the government shuts down. You see, I don't know what to tell you. May be by the time this report gets to Washington DC there may be less work load. But I can assure you that that may not be the case. The people in

Washington DC are suckers. Look Gabriel I don't know what to tell you.

Gabriel: I think am going to DC to file a complaint with the local police there. What do you think?

FBI Agent: The FBI is unlike the local police. The latter are quick and direct. If you commit a crime today you can get thrown in jail today while the local police work on the processes of prosecuting you. That is not the case with the FBI. We have to do a thorough investigation for the United States Justice Department. Sometimes it may take years to get any concrete answer. Finally the U. S. attorneys decide whether or not to prosecute. So if you go to DC local police I don't know what they can do. But I can assure you the FBI may not do anything about your complaint. That is the honest truth. But I am going to see if my secretary can type this out today or later. I shall get in touch with you later if I need more information. But it seems to me that you can sue the man in a civil court. Sometimes the courts entertain some cases even 7 years or more old. So you may want to try that. For at the FBI we only concentrate on more serious complaints or serious cases. Eventually we might work our way down the ladder to less important case like yours but I doubt it. Your case is even more complicated by the fact that you are a Nigerian. Most Nigerians in the USA have a bad reputation. That is not saying that all Nigerians are bad. For instance the last time I went to the Middle East I heard some people say " eh, he's an American, the Americans are not good…" I said to myself, well, this people cannot be referring to all Americans like that. Every American has his/her different ways. Anyhow, may be Mr. Lake had been defrauded by some Nigerians in the past and he Mr. Lake decided now to get even with another Nigerian. Unfortunately you and your brother happen to fall into that trap. Too bad! You see there is very little the FBI can do about that.

Gabriel: I called Mr. Lake today to let him know that I reported the case to the FBI and he told me he is getting a lawyer.

GBI Agent: You shouldn't have let him know about the FBI involvement. The truth you should know now is that the FBI is not going to investigate this matter further. One of the reasons is because the money involved is very little: only $120,000! Looks like a civil matter to me. I still can't see the fraud in it. I am not trying to defend Mr. Lake; I am just playing double advocate, trying to figure out Mr. Lake's defenses. But I am going to dictate this fact to my secretary to type it out. I shall proof read it whenever I can. But I can assure you nothing is *going to come out of this. The people at the FBI office in Washington DC will surely pass this by. That is my guess. May be I am wrong. I don't know. I shall retire in eleven months. See, I am 55 years old! Look Gabriel, I don't know what to tell you.*

Gabriel: Sir, I am very, very upset about all these rigmarole.

FBI Agent: What can I do? I am going to try to get this report to Washington DC. Let me tell you Gabriel I cannot jump thru all the stages that I need to go thru. I have been doing this for over 30 years and I retire in about 11months! I don't know how to explain this to you anymore. I don't even know if am going to get my paycheck for talking with you here. You see Gabriel there are inherent problems. Such is life you know.

Gabriel: So, now, what can I do to get the money back?

FBI Agent: You can sue him in a civil court. Some courts allow up to 7 years to entertain such complains. Or you can simply hope that the FBI would work on your case.

Gabriel: So, in these days and times, can somebody in this United States of America be saved from being defrauded of his/her hard earned money? Even if it is only $120,000?

FBI Agent: Yes, of course! If you are smart enough to know all the loopholes in the system you can even get away with murder, or theft involving millions of dollars. It is unfortunate but it is real. There have been thousands of cases that I have worked on only to be thrown out by the U. S. attorneys on grounds of legal technicality. That is why we also demand for complete detail and all evidences relating to the situation. In your case there are inherent problems. May be this guy called William Lake didn't mean to defraud you of $120,000 but couldn't help the situation that led him being unable to refund the money. May be he has only used part of that money. May be we can still recover some or most of the money. May be this guy is a genuine guy. May be this guy is a fake guy. May be this guy is an innocent guy. May be this guy is as guilty as charged. May be this guy will be willing to settle this matter peacefully. May be he is ready for a fight. These are some of the things I need to find out about Mr. Lake.

Gabriel: The sum of $120,000 must be refunded back no matter what ok!

FBI Agent: Let's hope so. I am going to try to type this report today. I might finish it tomorrow. I might forward it to my supervisor next day. Hopefully Washington DC may have it in a couple of months or so. The rest is a mystery. Your complaint may get dumped in the trash in Washington DC. It may get lost in the piles of other complaints in Washington DC, and so on and so forth.

Gabriel: Would you need anything more from me to help quicken the process of criminal action against Mr. William Lake?

FBI Agent: For now I am just going to call the BBB in Washington DC to request for more information.

Gabriel: Mr. Thompson at the BBB in Washington DC told me you can subpoena all or any record(s) relating to Mr. Lake/INTRANCO, and that the BBB is ready and willing to release all those records relating to Mr. Lake.

FBI Agent: We don't subpoena records. We just investigate. It is then left to the lawyers and the courts to handle the rest of the job. In your particular case we only have sketchy details. That can create problems. I just wish Murphy your brother could come over right away and give me all details. Hopefully the government wouldn't close down again, especially at the time when we are ready to deal with Mr. Lake.

Gabriel: Please give me couple of days to get more information and more records from Murphy to you. The bottom line though is to get the money from Mr. Lake.

FBI Agent: We might not prosecute Mr. Lake because of your complaint. But we might get him on some other grounds. So just chill and let us do our job. I am going to try to have this report by closing time today or tomorrow. I am also looking forward to my retirement in about eleven months or so. I am going to start on this complaint now. Please make copies of all relevant documents and bring them to the receptionist for onward transmission to me. May be I am not going to do anything about your case...

Gabriel: William Lake took $120,000 and refused to refund it. He said he was exporting fish from Chile/Peru waters, when in fact the fish from those waters had been contaminated according to a report in The Economist of February 23, and many other sources. When contacted about this worrisome fact and when asked to produce any document or evidence from the World Health Organization or from the Governments of Chile/Peru that fish from their waters was safe for consumption, Mr. Lake refused. Would the FBI allow African countries to be used as a dumping ground for contaminated fish and all kinds of fraudulent activities by companies in the United States? Is this fair sir?

FBI Agent: I understand your frustration. I also agree with you that such a thing is very bad. It is not fair. But, eh, such is life! The Nigerians in the United States and in many countries overseas have not been very honest too. You see, I am not trying to defend Mr. Lake; I am just trying to play double advocate. The Nigerians here or most of them have committed all kinds of crimes and gotten away with them. Now, does your brother, Murphy, have anything in the form of a contract signed by him and Mr. Lake or by representatives of INTRANCO, to which Mr. Lake is the director?

Gabriel: I don't know. But I think my oldest brother, Murphy, is too smart to send $120,000 to a guy in Washington DC merely thru telephone conversations and telemarketing tactics. However, I shall find out and let you know in due course. (In fact, dear readers, I later discovered that there was no contract signed by my brother and Mr. Lake or any agent of both parties. The whole deal was consummated and agreed upon via friendly hand shakes, telephone conversations and verbal agreement and the like. There was never any official contract signed, sealed and delivered. It was unbelievable!)

FBI Agent: Sometimes there are bad businesses or bad businessmen. Mr. Lake may be the worse crook on the surface of this earth but the FBI must have concrete facts to him to stop that. The worst thing we don't want to do is to start something against Mr. Lake when we know we wouldn't be able to finish it successfully. If your brother, Murphy, actually sent $120,000 to Mr. Lake without any contract in writing, signed, sealed and delivered, then, that is the dumbest thing I have ever heard of in my life! Nonetheless, the FBI can still investigate and get Mr. Lake to stop that if all he is doing is deceiving people to wire money to him when he knows he cannot deliver the goods he promised. On the other hand Mr. Lake can simply claim that he delivered the goods but that Murphy and his company refused *to accept them. So there are inherent problems. Look Gabriel I just don't know what to tell you.*

Gabriel: If Mr. Lake says he has the goods he collected $120,000 for, then where are the goods or the frozen fish?

FBI Agent: I don't know. That is going to be part of our investigation. You see Gabriel, we have got to be able to find out from Mr. Lake his own version or part of the whole deal. May be he didn't know the fish he was trying to export to Africa was contaminated. Even when these facts were revealed to him perhaps he had already paid for the fish and paid for all the arrangements for the freight. But, perhaps, he knew but tried to conceal those facts. In fact, perhaps the fish he was trying to export was already declared by the governments of Chile/Peru to be bad for consumption, and this guy, Mr. Lake, volunteered to destroy them free of charge; in which case he got the fish free of charge, and thereafter arrange to ship it to the innocent buyers in Africa. You see, there are so many possibilities or probabilities to your case. Perhaps Mr. Lake told the owners of the bad fish that he needed them for manure, or for non – human consumption. Therefore I am going to take a look at the publication which says the waters of Chile/Peru were contaminated in February, and investigate that further ok.

Certainly if there are reports at the time in question that people were dying for eating fish from the waters of Chile/Peru, then your brother, Murphy, should be entitled to bail out of the contract and get his money back. I shall investigate that very closely.

Gabriel: Sometimes life could be very funny. Can you believe that this man called William Lake would collect $120,000 for almost 5 years and pretends nothing is wrong with that ethically or otherwise. He goes about his business in Washington DC as if nothing is wrong. Why? Look, I am getting very upset. I need an answer, I mean positive answer now. Otherwise I shall go to Washington DC and get the local police there to hunt Mr. Lake down. I shall not sleep until every dime is paid by Mr. Lake. Sir I need the help of the FBI to get this assignment done peacefully.

FBI Agent: Why don't you go and get the remaining materials to me so that I can start on the report today. Although I cannot guarantee immediate result but I can at least guarantee all the processes before the report(s) leaves Denver to Washington DC: First I must have my secretary type it up. Thereafter I shall proofread it; thence to my supervisors; from there to my bosses in the 2nd floor; from there to the undersecretary on the 8th floor; from there to the assistant manager on the 9th floor; from there to the boss on the 10th floor; from there to the boss on the 11th floor; from there to the boss on the 13th floor...and finally to the boss on the 18th floor; from there back to the first floor for final checking and approval...

Gabriel: Ok, ok...I am going to my office to get some of the documents faxed to me today from overseas by my brother, Murphy. I shall come back here within two hours or so to enable you commence on the processes on investigation as par the FBI style ok.

FBI Agent: (both of us standing up to part for the day, can you believe that this FBI guy spent another 30 minutes or more to sum up the processes of investigation at the FBI again!) style ok.

FBI Agent: (both of us standing up to part for the day, can you believe that this FBI guy spent another 30 minutes or more to sum up the processes of investigation at the FBI again!) You see Gabriel I have just decided to start the paper work on the 17th floor. You know I shall retire in about 11 months or so. Up till now I have given all my life to the service of the FBI. 30 years of service, isn't that great Gabriel! Perhaps the government will shut down anytime I don't care. I am going to put this message thru on the computer right away. Whatever happens to the report when it gets to Washington DC is none of my business. Oh gush! I hate Washington DC! I am going to my office now. I shall try to do the best I can with the report. Anyway, I think I need to start on the 17th floor. From there I shall send it to the 18th floor for proofreading; from there to the 1st floor; from there to the 2nd floor; from there to the 3rd floor; from there to the 4th floor; from there to the 5th floor; from there to the 6th floor; from there to the 7th floor; from there to the 8th floor; from there to the 9th floor; from there to the 10th floor; from there to the 11th floor; from there to the 12th floor; from there to the 13th floor; from there to the 14th floor...

To Jackson for approval

To John for proof reading

To James for supervision

To Susan for reporting

To eh, Peter, for correction

To Margaret for packaging

To Mary for sorting

To Logan for mailing…etc.

Meanwhile the FBI motto says:

"Fidelity, bravery, and integrity".

Indeed.

Take good care of yourself, eat balanced diet, lots of fruits and vegetables, and drink water daily, exercise daily, please fall in love have good sex more frequently, keep good friends who are ready to be educated and work hard in life to enjoy their lives, be friendly with everyone regardless of race, gender, ethnicity, greed or religion, make everyone your friend and your family, give to the poor always, help the needy always, be the first to say hello to friends and strangers, be smart and stay away from trouble always, talk less, listen more, better yourself daily, improve your life daily, forgive always, respect and protect girls and women always, laugh daily and be around happy people, do humor, take life easy, enjoy life while it lasts, go out and get the millions of dollars waiting for you, since no one is born to be poor, get education and seek information daily, be rich in morality, do those things that are excellent, and have lots, and lots of fun! Bye!

HOW TO BE A GREAT LEADER AND A GREAT MANAGER BOTH AT THE WORK PLACE & AT HOME (PART 3)

PART THREE (NOTE: SO MANY SERIES COMING IN THE FUTURE)

By Prince Gabriel

Hon. Member US Army, MBA, Doctorate in Management

JD Candidate

Copyright © Prince Gabriel 2010

PREAMBLE

I served with HONORS in the United States Army. Throughout my service in the US Army I maintained ethical conduct and integrity in everything I did. I maintained strict discipline in everything in life: starting from when I woke up around 4.30 am till when I went back to bed around 7.30pm. I treated my colleagues justly and fairly, never cheated anyone, always worked very hard in life to earn everything I have, hitherto, and was always the first to help anyone in need or in distress, etc. That was how I earned my HONORS. I am here to share my leadership experiences with you with the hope you might like to do everything in your organization or in your country within a similar ethical conduct and maintain integrity in all your doings. I hope that is not asking too much of you, in order for you to become a great leader and a great manager, both at the work place and at home.

As an American Soldier, I have been trained to do what is right or what is excellent at all times, even when no one is watching me. As an American Soldier, I will always consider moral excellence, and the Rule of Law in whatever I do. **<u>I always consider Human Rights and try to be fair to everyone regardless of any circumstances I find myself</u>**. I will always comply with all rules and regulation at all times. There is simply no excuse for not doing the right thing, period! That, in a nutshell, is how to become a great manager, both at the work place and at home. Are you still interested in becoming a great manager and a great leader?

Now, **this idea of ethics and/or ethical conduct in everything we do ought to start at an early age.** It becomes extremely difficult when you are grown. If you have not been practicing ethics and integrity all your life, that is, doing what is legally and morally right at all times, without fear or favor, you have a lot of work to do to enable you become a great leader and a great manager. You need to start right now! Yes, you can!

Great managers, great leaders and great parent, are qualities we all have from the day we were all born. Now, we all can choose to nurture our leadership skills, through education, skill training, through personal efforts by reading a lot of books, asking a lot of questions, and by employing the power of thinking, and thereby becoming more creative and innovative on a daily basis; or we can choose to keep our skills from birth. Either way everyone out there is capable of being a great manager, a great leader and a great parent, both at the work place and at home. The most important thing is to keep thinking: never stop thinking. Think. Think and innovate something new daily. Think creatively. Create something or lots of things in your lifetime that is unique only to you. Think of something good, write it down and publish it, build something, license it in your name, etc. Think.

Reach out and touch somebody's life at work or at school today. Shake somebody's hand today, somebody you have never met before. Ask that person how he/she is doing. Smile. Be genuine in your feelings of friendship. Be humane. Talk about your families, the good and the bad, to get that person to open up. Be natural. Such is the hallmark of a great leader. Practice it daily. Pass it on.

At the end of every day, evaluate everything you have done for the day and get independent people to also help you evaluate it to see what or how you could have done things better. Always do a follow-up and make corrections and take the necessary actions next time to do it better and improve significantly, alright.

Above all, keep putting oil in your lamp and keep it burning daily, and never, ever allow the oil in your lamp to dry out: just keep the lamp burning for as long as you live. That is what great managers do daily. That is what great leaders do daily. That is what great men and women, boys and girls are doing daily: improving their lives on a daily basis; getting better and better at school, at work, in colleges, and universities and in your behaviors and attitudes, etc. Yes, you can!

CHAPTER ONE

COACH THE KIDS IN ETHICS & LET THEM GROW UP WITH IT

We have an obligation to train all our children while they are still young to do what is right always, and watch them, guide them, and train them strictly to grow up doing what is right, fair, legally and morally right at all times. Catch them young otherwise it might be too late, people! All parents and guardians should please raise and nurture all our children on the right path of life: honesty, hard-work, study hard and earn good grades, telling the truth at all times, without fear or favor, helping the poor and the needy, being patient and standing in lines and taking turns, teaching children to listen more and talk less, teaching children to be polite and to respect everyone, teaching kids to be fair at all times and to treat everyone equally and with dignity, teaching kids to be generous and selfless, and above all, teaching kids to be humane to others. Again, catch the kids young and train them rigorously on the right path of life outlined above, otherwise, it might be too late, ok!

There is no amount of education later in life that would change the mid of a crook and a greedy person like Bernard Madoff and his types from committing frauds or crimes. Sometimes, though, the kind of training in the US Army might go a long way to helping the criminals and greedy adults make a permanent turnaround for the better, if only these criminals and greedy people would enlist in the US Army! The training in the US

Army is perhaps the ultimate training to get future leaders, managers, executive and future Presidents of our nations to think straight, think clearly and logically, stay focused; and never be afraid to do the right thing, legally and morally.

More so, as a result of global conflicts and several conflicts already boiling everywhere around the globe, from Israel to Pakistan, to Iran to Russia, to North Korea, to China, and so on; as a result of these conflicts, that might inevitably lead to a Third World War, it is my recommendation here that future leaders, managers and Presidents of our nations should and ought to have some form of military trainings to be able to stay calm and able to determine the right course of action when major war breaks out. I hope somebody is listening!

CHAPTER TWO

EDUCATING THE KIDS AND YOUTHS, OUR FUTURE LEADERS

No nation can survive and prosper if its children and youths are wasting away on the streets without proper education and/or proper nurturing, a situation that is common in almost all Third World countries like Nigeria, Sierra Leone, and so on. When kids do not bond with society, they bond with criminals and terrorists, like the people recruited in Saudi Arabia and from Afghanistan by the terrorist groups to destroy the United States on 9/11/2001.

The best leaders and managers we can train to better manage our organizations and our nations in the future effectively and efficiently, and with less wars and conflicts in our lives, by inculcating the values of respect, equality, fairness, justice, equity and good conscience and of course, **WORLD PEACE**, are the children and youths out there today and tomorrow!

Most importantly, the female or girls among are children should be given equal chance with the male counterparts to be trained to manage and lead our organizations more effectively and efficiently into the 21st century and beyond. Evidence shows the men have been in power for centuries hitherto, and possess most of the authorities in the United States, Russia, China, Africa and most part of Europe, and have never been able to lead our organizations and our nations prudently, without economic meltdown, like the current great recession and countless wars and conflicts all over the world! Perhaps, it is time to give our young girls and women, who are well educated and very smart, like their male counterparts, or better in some cases, to become the next great managers, the next great leaders, and the next great Presidents of the United States, of Russia, China and of the United Nations! What do you think? How about a change?

CHAPTER THREE

FUN PROGRAMS TO KEEP OUR FUTURE LEADERS SAFE

Our young children and youths must be given every opportunity to be in school and colleges to be well trained in quality schools. Every young child or every youth MUST be allowed to attend the university freely or the government and all businesses and religious bodies MUST finance ALL young people to obtain good, marketable skills in the universities, to prevent crimes. Thereafter, jobs and business opportunities MUST be created for them by ALL the governments and nations of the world, period! Anything short of that will resort in crime and all sorts of problems in society like moral decadent, juvenile delinquency, etc.

Youths should be given the chance to bond with something productive always, both at home and after school programs like sports, swimming, volley ball, basket ball, soccer ball, cooking lessons, etc. The expenses for all these recreations should be paid by the government, businesses and religious bodies in our society. Please!

Ethics and moral right should be taught both at home when our kids are still very young and at all schools in every nation of the world. It is a must, if our civilization must survive and thrive in the future

I am begging every nation of the world and every one of you out there to put hands together to help our young children and our youths currently not being properly trained and provided for, to help reverse the situation for the better. Parents and guardians please wake up and spend more time with your child/children, read for them, visit their schools to help the teachers in every way possible, parents please teach your children the right way of life, teach them to be honest, to help people, to be polite with people and to do all those things that are excellent only. Please!!!

Teachers and politicians and Army personnel and all the good people in our society, especially our teachers should please teach more than the basics. Please teachers. I thank all our teachers and professors for their great work hitherto. The governments of all nations should please increase teachers' salaries. Please increase teachers' salaries. Please do everything to make our teachers and professors happy. When everyone in society is well educated and given great opportunities for better life, there would be less crime. That is a truism!

The standard of education in technologically advanced countries like Japan, Germany, and in the United Kingdom ought to be the same standard in Nigeria, Ghana, Sierra Leone, and in every developing country of the world. We have been giving less and less education to children in developing countries and minority children in the United States for too long! It must stop now!

If the crime rate in the United States and in Nigeria and South Africa must be reduced then all children and their parents must be given a fair, balanced access to the best universities and job opportunities or business opportunities. The time for fairness, justice, equity and respect for others is now. I think that is probably one of the best ways or the very best way to reduce crime and disorderly conducts in our life. I hope somebody is listening!

The young children and youths in Saudi Arabia are very angry because of unemployment and lack of quality education in a country so rich with crude oil. A lot of these youths were recruited to destroy America by the terrorists on 9/11/2001.

Youths and young children in the United States have access to too many illegal drugs and guns. Please replace those guns with books, and nice clothes, ok!

A lot of the youths in Nigeria have no education and are unemployed in a country so rich with crude oil and other natural resources.

Again, please help our children and youths in every way possible to enable them be well educated and help them to earn good money and good life and for our kids today to become the next great managers and the next great leaders, the next great parent and the next great Presidents of tomorrow: for our children and youths are the means through which we reproduce and preserve the best of ourselves. Thank you and God bless you!

Take good care of yourself, eat balanced diet, lots of fruits and vegetables, and drink water daily, exercise daily, please fall in love have good sex more frequently, keep good friends who are ready to be educated and work hard in life to enjoy their lives, be friendly with everyone regardless of race, gender, ethnicity, greed or religion, make everyone your friend and your family, give to the poor always, help the needy always, be the first to say hello to friends and strangers, be smart and stay away from trouble always, talk less, listen more, better yourself daily, improve your life daily, forgive always, respect and protect girls and women always, laugh daily and be around happy people, do humor, take life easy, enjoy life while it lasts, go out and get the millions of dollars waiting for you, since no one is born to be poor, get education and seek information daily, be rich in morality, do those things that are excellent, and have lots, and lots of fun! Bye!

HOW TO BE A GREAT LEADER AND A GREAT MANAGER BOTH AT THE WORK PLACE & AT HOME (PART 4)

PART FOUR (NOTE: SO MANY SERIES COMING IN THE FUTURE)

By Prince Gabriel

Hon. Member US Army, MBA, Doctorate in Management

JD Candidate

PREAMBLE

A great manager is that person who pays attention to details and knows what to do, when, where, why, and so on. She/he has a lot of experiences about that particular operation in question, and can handle anything that comes her way. She/he has been around doing the same thing for a while and knows every tiny little detail to be able to train her/his subordinates on the job. Above all, a great manager is very flexible, well educated, forward-looking, operates at little cost and brings in a lot of revenues or profits, very progressive and productive; and has earned her/his authority for knowing almost everything to know about the job, period! For instance, a great bank manager, or a great grocery store manager would open up her/his branch of operation about five or ten minutes before the official opening time, and would close her/his branch about 15 minutes after the official time for closing for the day has elapsed. Every child coming to the bank or store gets a candy or something nice and memorable and reminds the parent to go back there to the bank or store. When a child likes your business, trust me, the parent is going to keep coming back! And when you get into the place, bank or store where there is a great manager/leader, there is always good music playing that everybody likes, to make everyone happy, singing along, dancing, yes, dancing!. That is only few of the signatures of a great manager! Are you a great manager yet? Yes, you can!

A great leader on the other hand knows a lot about the manager's job, or ought to know a lot about the manager's job (like Jack Welch with a Ph.D. in Engineering and went through series of management job before ultimately earning the top job at General Electric!). But, a great leader is the visionary (the one with great foresight about the future and how to get there productively, prudently and at the speed of light!) and/or touch-bearer of any organization or nation. The leader helps to shape the internal Constitution or by-laws or rules or *Mission* of the *Organization,* or *Nation* which essentially gives a clear explanation and direction of where and what the Organization or Nation is going to be doing or producing to achieve its goals. The leader must be very healthy and agile, and has to be able to carry the touch-light of the organization or nation and let the light shine for everyone to see and be able to find their way through, in the tumultuous journey to the future, with her/him fully awake, alert on the wheel, and must know the right ways to journey through in a murky cloud to avoid too many bumps or fatal accident. A great leader possesses the best telescope to see every star in the milky-way galaxy! A great leader is very, very flexible and she/he is never afraid to ask questions or to ask for help, even from her/his subordinates. A great leader solicits for suggestions every time and values every suggestion, no matter how silly, and rewards everyone equally and fairly.

CHAPTER ONE

Specific things to help you become a great manager/leader

CHARACTERISTICS OF GREAT LEADERS & MANAGERS

1. **A great leader is like water**. Water cleans. A great leaders cleans her/his workers and not otherwise. We need water to survive: a great leader (or a good leader for that matter), brings water for every employee to quench their thirst and help the employees to survive, thrive and be well nourished and well nurtured. A great leader helps everyone to be happy and better off the position the employee was before joining the organization or nation. A

good leader and manager must therefore try to make life better for everyone, period!

2. **A great leader is like a fatherly figure or a motherly figure**: just imagine what it would be like if going to the work place is like going home to your home or to meet mom and dad! Even in the worst case scenario where a worker or some workers are not getting alone, or somebody is always creating problems (such a worker is called bottleneck) just being a jerk at the workplace: a great manager or leader treats that worker with love, not hatred, and cleans that worker until all the iniquities are cleansed and washed off by the leader *through effective communication and human-touch*, thereafter, the once troubled worker would become the best employee around, consistently! Note this fact: if that troublesome

employee is young, look for a young manager or a young person to try to reason with him/her and vice versa. Try and go up or down the age level and see with the employee. Work with the employee, and not terminate him/her. Compromise and cooperate with people. Every employee is a good employee or a good person, alright. Do you have what it takes to be a great manager and a great leader? Could you please learn it daily, practice it daily until you perfect it, and keep improving daily henceforth. Please!

3. **A great leader/manager is one who knows thy self**: do you know yourself? Honestly, do you really, really know yourself? If you know your capability and shortcomings, you can do something to better improve yourself daily. Please "know thy-self," as rightly pointed out by Plato.

4. **Do you know where you are coming from, and where you are going to?**

That is a very important question every great manager and leader should be asking herself or himself every second of the day. That is one of the best lessons I learned from the United States Army: to be well disciplined about everything in life; be well focused, and to pay attention to details. For instance, if you do not know where you are coming from, how on earth can you know where you are going to in life, for goodness sake! So, pay attention to details my friend! Read everything over and over again; make sure you understand something very well before you sign your life away, ok! PAY ATTENTION TO DETAILS!

5. **Great customer service: exceed the customer's expectation!**

    A good manager and a good leader would always do whatever it takes to satisfy the customer or client beyond her/his expectations. First find out what the customer/client want, as long as the customer's want or need is legal, please go the extra mile to make that customer/client very happy for a repeat business in the future, alright. You cannot go wrong for being flexible like water. Remember, water is fluid and flexible. Water cleans. You do the same, alright!

6. **A good manager or leader is humane and treats others with respect.**

This is, perhaps, one of the greatest qualities a good leader and a good manager must possess and act on daily. It means you must love your fellow human beings the same way you love yourself. You cannot fake genuine love and feelings toward your fellow human being. You can pretend you love people when in fact you do not. You can lie to love somebody, but your actions and body language would say otherwise. So, be truthful. Be honest. Even when you really don't love or care for someone, try, please try very hard and help that person, anyway. Please try. Wish your enemy well. The moment you can help your enemy and wish your enemy well, you have reached the apex of moral excellence! The leaders and managers and people out there who can help their enemies or those they do not like, as soon as you cultivate that habit of helping people you do not like very much, you will be blessed forever! Trust me here ok! I speak to you as an American Soldier.

It means you must not fart the air or pollute the environment when somebody is eating food nearly. It means you must be fair and just at all times and be nice, generous and kind. Yes, be kind, and practice kindness daily!

7. **Demand quality work or service at all times from your employees and reward your employees through pay increase, surprise gifts, etc**

Yes, great managers and leaders must lead by example: show your people how quality (and quantity) things can be produced efficiently *at less costs* then guide and supervise everyone to reach their goals successful; and always praise little achievements until everyone succeeds. DO NOT SHOUT OR CHASTISE OR PUT DOWN YOUR EMPLOYEES OR SUBORDINATES IN ANY FORM OR SHAPE, for goodness sake! Be social, be humane and respectful of others who may be slow to learn or comprehend. Try to understand and act like a blood family to your worker, even when that person is not related to you in any form or shape. Be there for them and help lift them up to the next level. Can you, please. Please. Please. That is the signature of a great manager, a great leader, or a good person! Can you please be like this great manager and great leader here? Yes, you can!

8. One of the greatest assets of a great manager and a great leader is to *talk less and listen more*. Yes, talk less, speak clearly; slow down for everyone to understand you, talk

less, put everything you say in writing and let everyone sign for it after reading and understanding you, in that way everyone is totally on board with you. So, talk less, listen more, and make sure you have a good joke or jokes every time you talk ok.

9. Ask for feedback always and do a follow-up on the feedback to make corrections; that is very, very important! Have an open door policy where anyone can get to you easily without any kind of hindrance whatsoever. Have one on one conversation, private talk with your employees, or family people daily or weekly to let them know how they are doing. If you are so busy, please send informal emails or text messages or a phone call to everyone. Communicate more often. Ask for a dinner or lunch time with your immediate, trusted employees or

family people more often. *Get the meetings of the mind going always where everyone understand what is going on;* and for goodness sake do not keep anyone in the dark, for that can betray trust and friendship built over the years. If you make mistake apologize immediately and give full and complete details and explanation without hiding anything from your workers or family member. Cultivate this habit and remain one of the best managers and leaders out there!

10. **SHARE THE WEALTH OF YOUR ORGANIZATION OR NATION EQUITABLY:** If you are making little or huge profits as a result of the team work and/or group work and cooperation and contributions from everyone in your organization, please, for goodness sake, share the wealth and huge profits equitably! Although, your workers or

family members may not be part owners of this little or huge profit legally, but naturally, or by the law of nature, your workers and family members, besides the shareholders or investors, are all part owners of any profits to your organization or nation. Please share any profits equitably to everyone who may have contributed to it directly or indirectly. If you can practice this great habit religiously, you have now reached the point where you can be called a great manager and a great leader! Yes, you can!

CHAPTER TWO

SPECIFIC THINGS YOU CAN DO AT HOME TO MAKE YOU A GREAT MANAGER/LEADER AT HOME

LOVE HEALS. LOVE IS HAPPINESS, AND HAPPINESS IS LOVE.

ARE YOU IN LOVE YET?

Love is selfless.

Love does not boast.

Love is not rude.

Love is fluid and flexible.

Love is like water, it cleans.

Love is not self-seeking.

Love does not delight in evil.

Love is good, always generous and considerate.

Love is not easily angered, love forgives quickly.

Love is forward-looking.

Love keeps no record of wrongs. Love is share-endurance, tight bond, love is discovery, gets better daily and lots and lots of fun together! Are you in love?

PRACTICAL THINGS YOU CAN DO FOR HAPPINESS ON A DAILY BASIS

1. Please fall in love and forever be happy, happy, happy!

2. Learn to laugh loud daily. Every time you have course to laugh, just laugh as loud as you can if it means you falling down on the ground, crying happily, bouncing your legs and hands- do it! A good laugh well expressed without any kind of restrictions will help your body, spirit and soul to be alive and well. Laughter is the best expression of happiness, no matter your physical or physiological problems, please laugh, laugh and laugh. Laughter is the best natural medicine to life's tumult. So, laugh away your sorrow. Laugh because you are beautiful. Laugh because life is beautiful. Laugh, laugh…

3. Learn how to sing daily, whether you know how to sing or nor, just sing, sing to people, sing to yourself, sing aloud, sing silently, just sing to yourself. Singing takes so many forms, you can hum, whistle or mime. Please do not let a day go by without singing. Sing, clap your hands…

4. Dancing. Put on your music and dance daily. Put on your favorite music or beat your drums. Whether you listen to music or not just dance daily. The moment you cultivate the habit of dancing daily, the sky is the limit. Please dance in the morning, dance in the afternoon, dance at night even when you are sleeping at night get up and dance! Dance and be lively always!

5. Everyone should fall in love and have a relationship in order to be happy. Do whatever you have to do attract a partner that you can fall in love with. The most important thing is that you should be thinking daily of somebody you truly like and love. A good friend or good lover that you can tell stories, sing, eat, laugh and go dancing with, a confidant. Every man or woman out there should be falling

in love and staying steadfast in love. Try to be passionate on a daily basis it is very, very essential for happiness!

6. Live a natural life on a daily basis, even if for only one hour. Learn to stay without electricity or the microwave, or anything artificial. Enjoy nature, feel the sun, take a walk on the beach, eat organic foods, stay quiet in the room without any music playing, or sit down and listen to the whistling birds and trees. Feel and enjoy nature more frequently, please.

7. Get involved with a least a sport in your life. It could be football, soccer, tennis, swimming, sex or golf with Tiger Wood! Just get busy with a sport or more.

8. Learn the habit of saying "Yes, I can do it" to every dream or goal you have. Whether you are in college or a new

profession, tell yourself that you can be successful. You will be successful! Trust me.

9. Whenever you come across any sharp object or pins on the ground or floor, pick it up and put it away in a trash. In other words, try to do favors to strangers every time even when no one has asked you, and without expecting anything in return. Be proactive in helping others.

10. Learn something new that you never knew before in your life daily. It could be reading a new book, cooking a new meal, looking up new information on the internet just learn something new daily.

11. Surprise a homeless or poor person with a large sum of money without letting your identity known to that person and just walk away, periodically.

12. Do something nice for children, at least once every week, it could be in the daycare, elementary school, charity or orphanage home, just do something for the children, at least once a week.

13. Surprise your mother or an elderly lady (please never call an elderly lady "old" lady in America or in Europe!) who is in need of help with a special gift at least once a month.

14. Are you getting enough sleep daily? Say six to eight hours of sleep daily. Please relax and cool your mind, body and soul. In order to be truly happy daily, you need all the sleep and rest you can get. You can check with your doctors to verify this important fact of life: please get good sleep, ok! Tips to getting good sleep: first eat good food, get exercise, then a bath, stay in a quiet, dark room, empty your mind of any thoughts, stay blank, relax, sometime soft classical music on very low volume, may help, stay quiet, shhhhh...

15. If you ever quarrel with anyone, or if you have any enemy, learn to make amends as quickly as possible. Just forgive and forget, even if it means losing some money or losing face or if it means you are cheated in some form, do not worry about it. For, if you let little trifles bother your life, your enemy has defeated you, even if you won a case against your enemy, or even if you are victorious in war or conflict, it does not matter! Please do not keep a protracted conflict. Do not keep enemy, period! The very fundamental tenet of happiness, or being happy, forbids enemy, period! Please try this idea and see what I mean.

Please apologize, give in, let go of that thing, and simply move on to more interesting thing, more rewarding thing in life, please! As the parable goes: if you see a naked, mad person running around naked on the street, do not run after that naked person, with yourself naked too; if you do, you become a mad person too! Got it? The message for some of the very best ways to manage the human affairs is coded in the Itsekiri language thus: ***ogba bi ireh owu agbadueyewe, etsuja ooo!*** It means for you to use rational behavior at all times, to be fair, just, and to use practical wisdom in dealing with your friends and foes alike, not war. I hope all the war mongers out there in America, Afghanistan, Iraq, Iran, North Korean, Israel, the Palestinians, etc, get the message now before it is too late!

Do all these things religiously, besides other things that you consider excellent in life and forget about being happy!

(Please read *The Book of Total Happiness*).

CHAPTER THREE

PROTECT YOUR FAMILY FROM THIEVES & CRIMINALS

Whether or not you burglar proof your home, a hundred percent protection from thief is impossible even if you live in a fortress like the current situation in Nigeria. However, some practical strategies below taken from dozens of tips old and new will get you at least 70 percent of the new way to total protection if you live in the Western World; since petty theft here in America and Western Europe are done mostly by the kids looking for money to buy drugs.

1. Keep a lived –in look. Burglars and thieves hate confrontations. According to the spokes woman for the national crime convention counsel and occupied home or one that looks more of the time constitutes the first line of defense. Pretend that there are people inside the home. A lived- in look is especially important during the day when burglarizing occurs especially when people are at work. This is usually between 8 am and 9am in the morning when all mothers are taking the kids to the school. Burglars and thieves know all the clues to an empty home. For instance, a newspaper on the porch or driveway in the middle of the day. An empty trash cans left unattended to or letters and mail still in the mail-box

and indoor lights left on all day. To prevent all this, please bring in the mail or have a mail slot where the mails are not hanging out for people to see. Do not leave your name inside or outside the door so that the thieves do not call you to check if you are in. Invest some little money to buy timers and light triggered devices that switch lamps and other appliances on and off to simulate a lived –in look. A lamp might be said to go in the family room late in the day for example, a timer might also control a radio tuned to a talk station playing loudly enough to be heard outside. These devices are available in most hardware and home improvement stores. Vacationers empty homes are a burglars bonanza, more home are broken into in August says the FBI than any other month. This is different if you live outside the United States. People away for long period should keep a car or a boat in the driveway. The grass should be mowed regularly. A neighbor or a trusted teenager should open the curtains or blinds in the morning or close them at night. Keep the air conditioning running during the summer and put out trash and take the cans in on collection day. In areas where call forwarding is available that is better than answering machines for extended periods of vacation. The call forward service automatically redirect incoming calls to any local or long distance number you designate or to a neighbor, a relative or to a phone at your vacation spot. Thieves and burglars will have no way of knowing that your phone is not being answered from your home.

2. Be an alarmist. Home securities systems are effective although expensive system to use. If you can install one, it will chase the thieves away because the presence of it is enough to send many burglars and thieves looking for easier places elsewhere.

3. Put on the dog. The dogs can be as effective as security system and many dogs are trained to bark at strange voices and quiet down when the stimulus is removed.

4. Know thy neighbor. Burglars hate watchful eyes. Police officers around the country have always

suggested getting to know your neighbor and to mutually agree to look for one another's homes. It is extremely important to know all your neighbors to easily identify a stranger or a thief.

The next step up might be to join or organize a neighborhood watch, a police community program that train citizens to report suspicious activities or strangers to the police.

5. Be vigilant. Most thieves just sneaks through an unlocked door, window or attached garage. The solution is to please lock your home and garage every minute you leave if only for a minute or two. Burglars are surprisingly very fast. The thieves specialize in robbing the house even when the owners

are outside having a barbecue. The thieves dashes in and grabs what he can, escaping while some people are outside mowing the grass while they are being distracted by the machine. It is good preventive measure to call local police to check out the security measures installed in your home and to get the police to check out any weak spots because the police have extensive training to cover all the security weak spots in your home.

6. Engrave all important items in your home and put special stamps that are permanent to prevent your items being sold and the police can help identify them. Never allow strangers into your home looking

for direction or pretending to be lost because they may be looking for things to steal.

Take good care of yourself, eat balanced diet, lots of fruits and vegetables, and drink water daily, exercise daily, please fall in love have good sex more frequently, keep good friends who are ready to be educated and work hard in life to enjoy their lives, be friendly with everyone regardless of race, gender, ethnicity, greed or religion, make everyone your friend and your family, give to the poor always, help the needy always, be the first to say hello to friends and strangers, be smart and stay away from trouble always, talk less, listen more, better yourself daily, improve your life daily, forgive always, respect and protect girls and women always, laugh daily and be around happy people, do humor, take life easy, enjoy life while it lasts, go out and get the millions of dollars waiting for you, since no one is born to be poor, get education and seek information daily, be rich in morality, do those things that are excellent, and have lots, and lots of fun! Bye!

HOW TO BE A GREAT LEADER AND A GREAT MANAGER BOTH AT THE WORK PLACE & AT HOME (PART 5)

PART FIVE (NOTE: SO MANY SERIES COMING IN THE FUTURE)

By Prince Gabriel

Hon. Member US Army, MBA, Doctorate in Management

JD Candidate

INTRODUCTION

Suppose you are given a little child or an infant to care for, would you rather have gotten some license or proper coaching on how best to be proactive to care for the child, like feeding the child at the right time, and not waiting until the infant *cries* for food, changing the diapers on time and not when it is super soaked, getting the child to nap at the right time? Or would you wait for the infant to be super hungry, after being starved for hours (I hope nobody out there is doing that to any child!), and after the diaper is super wet for hours?

Suppose there is an infant or a little baby *crying* and would not stop crying, the doctor is called and feels nothing is wrong with the child medically, yet the little child just keep crying: whaaaaa!!!!!

What would you do to calm the little child down and keep the child quiet or to go to sleep? You cannot concentrate to do anything productive since the little child crying uncontrollably is *stressing* you and you must do something very fast to resolve the crying baby's needs and wants before you can really be productive again. What would you do and how?

Well, after trying everything like giving the baby a shower, feeding the baby, diming the light, singing a lullaby; and none of that seems to work the little child is still crying whaaa, you can ignore the baby and hope the baby would cry and go to sleep while you continue doing whatever you are doing under this stressful condition.

Or you can try another trick, take the baby out for a walk for a fresh air or take the baby out in your car, for a nice ride around town, and see the magic of that trick working well for you!

How many lessons can you learn from this story? What is the moral of this story? Please, think.

CHAPTER ONE

BEING PROACTIVE & FINDING BETTER WAYS TO IMPROVE BEFORE DISASTER HIT

Specific things you can do to be proactive and keep improving are:

1. Hire or employ smart and creative people, from all works of life. *Intelligent and creative people who are useful and productive* would definitely help you to figure out how best to think proactively and become better and better daily.

2. Also, hire some not so smart and creative people, but who are well educated, and are beautiful, attractive, like beautiful girls and boys, men, and women, who have

connections and/or know how to start and finish any project successfully; and can get things done very well.

3. Send out your workers and managers out as "mystery shoppers or investigators" to other organizations or nations that are doing well, find out specific things they are doing well and how they are doing it so well, copy it, improve on it, without breaking any law, and modify it to fit your culture, customs, traditions or environment. This is extremely important if you want to stay ahead of the game, prosper and survive in the future! I hope somebody is listening!

4. Get good sleep daily. Rest well. Learn daily. Learn something new and creative daily. ***You have got to be the best hustler ever out there if you must be proactive*** *and be prosperous and/or productive in a sustainable way into the future ad infinitum.*

5. Always have huge cash saved somewhere to acquire properties and wealth from people, organization or countries in trouble or to expand into new opportunities after doing a thorough feasibility study, or as a safeguard for rainy days. Have a Research and Development (R&D) Department staffed with the most intelligent, smartest, honest (yes, honest people with integrity!) and the most creative people anywhere who knows every Information Technology (IT) out there and how best to put them into use for your benefits and productivity. Look my people: that is exactly what Microsoft is doing today. That is exactly what Google is doing daily. That is exactly what China is doing as a

country. That is exactly what Brazil is doing as a country. However, that is exactly what Nigeria is *not* doing! I hope somebody is listening!

6. ***Always move prudently, diligently, but at the speed of light***, at the same time! If there is anything stressing you out, take care of it quickly and take necessary ACTIONS, (yes, ACTIONS!) to get things done productively. The kind of politics in the so-called democratic system in the United States, India, Nigeria, and so on, should and must be modified in such a way to give the President of these countries (who must be well educated in how to manage and lead, be certified by medical doctors as having good health before taking office!) the executive authorities quickly in the economic front to take quick initiatives to move these countries forward, prudently,

diligently, but at the speed of light! That is exactly what is happening in Brazil where the Constitution of Brazil gives the President of that country an executive authority to get certain initiatives done (on the economic front) after consulting with his smart teams, within six months without the kind of arguments and counter-arguments in Washington DC that leads to nothing, and the Legislators or members of Congress in Brazil simply approve without questioning, within that six months period or short period of economic initiatives and productivity. China with its group of smart and extremely intelligent rulers are doing exactly the same thing, getting economic matters resolved quickly and moving that country forward at the speed of light, albeit, human right abuses and the Rule of Law are major issues in the Chinese system. The United States, India, Nigeria and other democratic system should please send "mystery shoppers and investigators" to China, India and Brazil and check out exactly what works, check out the educational system in China and India, in terms of Science and Technology, how the rulers and governments there in China and Brazil are not arguing too much like in Washington DC, but taking quick economic initiatives in a cooperative manner and perhaps copy and improve on them. Everybody is stealing from everybody there is no shame in that!

7. Do you speak in the language (s) and cultures of your organization or nation?

No organization or nation can hope to improve and grow and become number one or become advanced in the sciences, technology or the arts if the major language(s) spoken in that organization or nation is/are a foreign language(s), period!

For instance, China is developing, and doing very well economically and educationally because the Chinese people have official languages that are indigenous to the people in China. The people in China (just like the Japanese people who fought successfully to chase away the Christians-Western countries and others from colonizing them and changing their languages, culture and traditions) are raised are nurtured with their cultures and traditions, the very essence of their lives. *All the children in China take a lot of pride in their languages and cultures and traditions, and they learn and master their languages and cultures first before later learning the English Language! So, everything taught in schools and universities are in their native languages and they understand it very well!* The same thing in Israel, Brazil, India, and *even South Africa has eleven official languages, which includes the native languages of black Africans!*

Nigeria, on the other hand, has the English Language, the language of the British people, has its official language! Whereas, Nigeria has a lot of indigenous languages, like Yoruba, Ibo, Hausa, Ijaw, Itsekiri, Calabar, and so many languages that have roots in Nigeria, *languages that are the very essence of the people of Nigeria, are not made official languages*, like you have in South Africa and elsewhere. That is perhaps, one of the major things pulling back country like Nigeria, from ever developing economically, educationally and otherwise. With all due respect to Nigerians, especially those who cannot speak any Nigerian language, if you do not know where you are coming from, if you do not know your traditions and cultures, if you do not understand your history, if you do not know who you are, your languages, cultures and traditions, if you do not know or understand from where you have come from, how can you understand where you are going to in life???

CHAPTER TWO

WHEN ALL SOLUTION FAILS, GO OUT FOR A FRESH AIR

As you can see from our baby crying uncontrollably from the introduction above, sometimes, the solution(s) you need to get things going again are given by nature: go out and take fresh air! Take a ride around town or travel overseas and see different things, amuse your minds with something new, perhaps, funny and interesting (perhaps take some wine to gladden the mind, rest and sleep for about ten hours and see the magic working for you!). Take your minds away from a quagmire something in a mess of some sort; get your mind into something fluid and flexible, something totally new, different and/or natural. Yes, visit nature, touch nature, and natural things, look up there at the stars at night, let the mind wander.

Go to another country and learn different languages and cultures. Go out and help people in need, be generous, give charities to the homeless and the poor. You will be surprised that in the course of doing good things and not focusing too much on your problems, solutions for moving your organization or nation forward will pop up naturally! Just try it and see the magic for yourself.

CHAPTER THREE

APPEAL TO EMOTION, CRY!

When all solutions fail, cry and beg people to help you out like our little infant in the introduction above! Well, you may think that a Chief Executive Officer (CEO) of an organization or the President of a country or the head of any organization crying is not serious. That is not true!

In fact, that was what Mr. Akio Toyoda, the president of Toyota in Japan did in 2010, after reading this book, when he cried publicly to show remorse for the death of innocent people killed during the Toyota pedal problems!

The fact is: an appeal to emotion by crying genuinely, honestly showing emotions and crying for solutions or help, whether, the cry is done by a man or a woman (although, women have more powers with their tears than we have with our guns!), something positive will almost always come out of it! Just try it and see the magic work for you!

Take good care of yourself, eat balanced diet, lots of fruits and vegetables, and drink water daily, exercise daily, please fall in love have good sex more frequently, keep good friends who are ready to be educated and work hard in life to enjoy their lives, be friendly with everyone regardless of race, gender, ethnicity, greed or religion, make everyone your friend and your family, give to the poor always, help the needy always, be the first to say hello to friends and strangers, be smart and stay away from trouble always, talk less, listen more, better yourself daily, improve your life daily, forgive always, respect and protect girls and women always, laugh daily and be around happy people, do humor, take life easy, enjoy life while it lasts, go out and get the millions of dollars waiting for you, since no one is born to be poor, get education and seek information daily, be rich in morality, do those things that are excellent, and have lots, and lots of fun! Bye!

HOW TO BE A GREAT LEADER AND A GREAT MANAGER BOTH AT THE WORK PLACE & AT HOME (PART 6)

PART SIX (NOTE: SO MANY SERIES COMING IN THE FUTURE)

By Prince Gabriel

Hon. Member US Army, MBA, Doctorate in Management

JD Candidate

INTRODUCTION

Euro Disney is the company that owns and operates Disneyland in Paris. Initially when Disney land went from the United States to Paris the company refused wine being served in Disneyland, Paris, as requested by the French customers in Paris, since the management in the parent company in the United States felt it was not the style in the United States; so, it would not allow it across the ocean in a different country! Can you believe that?

So the French customers refused to attend Disneyland in Paris, and the company lost a lot of money! You would think with all the education and experiences of top management that Disneyland could not have made such a silly mistake, well, it did!

It took some years before management of Disneyland decided to put into action the business *dictum* "go global, but act local".

So, as a good manager or good leader, you ought to find out what the local customs and the laws and usages of the local place of your business or organization are, and for goodness sake follow or practice those customs and regulations if you want to survive and thrive as a business or nation, alright!

Now, the next thing here is how to market your business or products or yourself without paying for advertising or promotional costs, using Information Technology (IT), word of mouth, etc.

Social media, online sources, word of mouth, are just few of the ways you can use to market your products or yourself freely and make tons of money in profits!

Now, this is very important: the difference between regular managers/leaders, and great managers/leaders are those who can market and promote their organization or nation well by all means necessary with little or no cost, while making huge profits. This is very true, my people!

Social media such as Face book, Twitter, LinkedIn, are tools you can use for the buzz and generate awareness about you and your products.

Another tool is WordPress where you can post a press release about yourself and/product for free! A well-designed website using WordPress can do the advertising for you for free!

Visit your website frequently and communicate with customers and clients via your social network more frequently to clarify what you are and your quality products at reasonable or less cost compared to others in the field. Please make sure you are honest about you truly having quality products and services, and since you know how to do marketing and promotions at little or no cost to you, you can now afford to lower your cost and make tons of money in profit.

CHAPTER ONE

HOW TO USE SOCIAL NETWORK FOR FREE PROMOTION

1. Set up a private and business accounts with Face book, two separate face book accounts. Use your business account in Face book to advertise for free. Look for all your real friends daily and add them. Within two months you should have thousands of friends who are also linked to other thousands of friends!

2. Sign up for Twitter and LinkedIn. Remember to write the name of all your products and services as you fill out the lines. That is how you advertise for free!

3. Use free tool like Twellow.com to find people in your areas or your community who may be using Twitter and follow as many people a day as you can and communicate with them about your products and services

4. Set up a free account at Hootsuite.com. Once you have done that you can update your information at Twitter, Face book, all at once, and promote your products and services for free there too!

5. First and foremost, get to know people and familiarize yourself, be nice, be social, be polite; thereafter, you can try to sell your products and services! Got it?

CHAPTER TWO

CREATIVE WAYS TO MARKET YOUR PRODUCTS FOR FREE

1. Suppose you are operating your goods and services in Brazil, you can print your name, organization, products, services, phone number, email and full contact information in a little soccer ball and simply give it away to little kids and adults alike all over Brazil! Soccer is one of the very best things Brazil is known all over the world for. See the logic there! If you are in the United States you can print your information in a base ball or American football and give it out in the same way alright. Do the same thing in countries all over the world and see the result.

2. You can also print your products and services and your information in a T-shirt, a dress or some nice, plain clothes and give it to the homeless, the poor and others in every Downtown or central places of business, in countries all over the world to wear daily for a little monthly pay or stipends to the homeless and poor people. This idea is extremely effective in marketing if it is done right. Here, you are helping the poor in a little way while marketing your products and services to the world at little or no cost to you.

3. You can use beautiful, funny school boys and girls (yes, very funny people!), men and women who are extremely good-looking, but not professional models, who can simply present themselves naturally in any professional games wearing your T-shirts and clothes every time all over the

world for little pay. That too can be extremely effective if it is done right with the consent and approval of the parents of kids all over the world.

4. You can team up with charitable organizations all over the world for little or no cost to you, contribute little money to charitable events and make arrangements to show case your products and services in an ethical way. Yes, in an ethical way, ok!

5. You can get your pretty school/college boys and girls to befriend or fall in love with media mogul or newspaper writers, editors and columnists to do a free write-up or cover on your products and services, in an ethical and legal way too!

6. You can always do some dramatic or sentimental things, like wide parties with free food and stuffs for college girls and boys willing to get naked and party all night long and get the press or media to cover it with your products and services at hand! So many creative, ethical ways you can do this you know!

7. There are thousands of free ads online you can use for free!

8. There are community bulletin all over the world you can write or type your products and services without paying a dime for it!

9. Have great products and services out there and word of mouth alone can spread the good news like a wide fire! For instance Harvard University and Oxford University are

some of the best universities in the world because the quality of education there is first class, period! As you can see here, **you do not even need to do anything to promote yourself if you can make the best thing in terms of quality, value, ethics, integrity, and so on; but most of all the highest quality stuffs, with the best in safety.**

10. As a great manager/leader, you need to take the necessary actions to do something good and productive for your community, for your nation and for the world. Do excellent things like, volunteering to help in after-school programs for children and youths in trouble, giving public speeches to study hard in schools, for kids to listen to their parents and teachers, avoid drugs, or teach them how to play soccer, how to cook delicious foods, safe exercise techniques, or to help the poor and needy, and so on.

Simply get involved in all activities that would give some net good to society in a positive and productive way. While there, if it is appropriate wear the T-shirt showing your products and services, and give some out freely!

As you can see here there are thousands of ways you can market and promote yourself, your business, your nation and your stuffs at little or no cost to you. ***Always think and find creative ways for promotions and marketing at little or no cost to you***. Good luck!

HOW TO BE A GREAT LEADER AND A GREAT MANAGER BOTH AT THE WORK PLACE & AT HOME (Part 7)

PART SEVEN (NOTE: SO MANY SERIES COMING IN THE FUTURE)

By Prince Gabriel

Hon. Member US Army, MBA, Doctorate in Management

JD Candidate

INTRODUCTION

Great managers and great leaders should carry their organizations or their nations across the Atlantic, to join their peers, as the very best among equals, in a global village, like Charles Lindberg did in 1927. In order to achieve this great feat, great managers and great leaders must learn and master the act or art of doing business at the least cost possible, ***reduce expenditures, re-use old stuffs or materials and recycle*** stuffs, while making huge profits. You have to employ the expertise of people who can help you cut cost down, make quality things and/or services to sell outside/overseas, while buying very little from outside/overseas. ***Again, great managers and leaders, please make more quality things to sell overseas, and buy less from overseas. Be self-sufficient at home***. Make quality stuffs and use your stuffs more without depending on others to make things for you. Thant is you become advanced technologically and scientifically. Is that too difficult to achieve?

Look around your organization or nation and identify wastes and eliminate it totally, if you must succeed in your flight across the Atlantic, ***since you need the least weight and lots of fuel***

for a successful flight across the Atlantic, just like Charles Lindberg did in 1927. Please read the story below to get a sense of what I am talking about here, then, think and write down how many lessons in leadership and management you may have learned from this great story.

7:52 A.M., May 20, 1927

At 7:52 A.M., May 20, 1927 Charles Lindbergh gunned the engine of the "Spirit of St Louis" and aimed her down the dirt runway of Roosevelt Field, Long Island. Heavily laden with fuel, the plane bounced down the muddy field, gradually became airborne and barely cleared the telephone wires at the field's edge. The crowd of 500 thought they had witnessed a miracle. Thirty-three and one half-hours and 3,500 miles later he landed in Paris, the first to fly the Atlantic alone.

Working as a mail pilot a year earlier he heard of the $25,000 prize for the first flight between New York and Paris. Backed by a group of St. Louis businessmen, Lindbergh supervised the building of his special plane and set out after the prize. Other teams were attempting the feat - some had met disaster. Lindbergh equipped himself with four sandwiches, two canteens of water and 451 gallons of gas. Midway through the flight "sleet began to cling to the plane. That worried me a great deal and I debated whether I should keep on or go back. I decided I must not think any more about going back."

On the evening of May 21, he crossed the coast of France, followed the Seine River to Paris and touched down at Le Bourget Field at 10:22P.M. The waiting crowd of 100,000 rushed the plane. "I saw there was danger of killing people with my propeller and I quickly came to a stop." He became an instant hero, "the Lone Eagle." New York City gave him the largest ticker tape parade ever, the president awarded him the Distinguished Flying Cross. His feat electrified the nation and inspired enthusiastic interest in aviation.

Takeoff

Bad weather and the prospect that his transatlantic flight would be delayed for a number of days greeted Lindbergh upon his arrival in New York. However, on May 19th, a favorable weather report predicted a break in the rain prompting Lindbergh to make his attempt the next day. He arrived at the airfield before dawn the next morning, prepared his plane for flight and began his historic journey:

Minnesota Historical Society Photo
http://www.mnhs.org

"About 7:40 A.M. the motor was started and at 7:52 I took off on the flight for Paris. The field was a little soft due to the rain during the night and the heavily loaded plane gathered speed very slowly. After passing the halfway mark, however, it was apparent that I would be able to clear the obstructions at the end. I passed over a tractor by about fifteen feet and a telephone line by about twenty, with a fair reserve of flying speed. I believe that the ship would have taken off from a hard field with at least five hundred pounds more weight. I turned slightly to the right to avoid some high trees on a hill directly ahead, but by the time I had gone a few hundred yards I had sufficient altitude to clear all obstructions and throttled the engine down to 1750 R.P.M. I took up a compass

course at once and soon reached Long Island Sound where the Curtiss Oriole with its photographer, which had been escorting me, turned back."

Darkness

Lindbergh continued his flight over Cape Cod and Nova Scotia and headed for the open Atlantic as darkness fell:

"Darkness set in about 8:15 and a thin, low fog formed over the sea through which the white bergs showed up with surprising clearness. This fog became thicker and increased in height until within two hours I was just skimming the top of storm clouds at about ten thousand feet. Even at this altitude there was a thick haze through which only the stars directly overhead could be seen. There was no moon and it was very dark. The tops of some of the storm clouds were several thousand feet above me and at one time, when I attempted to fly through one of the larger clouds, sleet started to collect on the plane and I was forced to turn around and get back into clear air immediately and then fly around any clouds which I could not get over."

PLEASE NOTE THE COST-SAVING IDEAS BELOW HERE

A small manufacturer, the Ryan Aeronautical Company of San Diego, agreed to build a plane for Lindbergh, for $6,000 plus the cost of the engine. He went to their small plant in San Diego and supervised the design modifications and the construction his monoplane. Essentially, the *Spirit of St. Louis* was a custom-built airplane, designed expressly to fly Lindbergh across the Atlantic. A. Scott Berg, in *Lindbergh*, called it a "two-ton flying gas tank." **Lindbergh sacrificed every possible bit of weight for more fuel capacity. No parachute, no radio, no brakes, not even a forward-facing window (a small periscope would do)**. Twenty-seven feet long, as the design evolved, the wings grew to forty-five feet, to help lift the 2700 pounds (400+ gallons) of gas. **The rest of the airplane, the engine, and its**

pilot only weighed about 2500 pounds. Powered by a state-of-the-art 223hp Wright Whirlwind J-5C engine, the plane could cruise for 4,200 miles. Ryan employees worked day and night to finish the aircraft in just two months. Its tail identified the aircraft as "N-X-211 RYAN NYP" "N" was the international aeronautical code for the United States. "X" stood for experimental. It was the 211th such licensed plane. "RYAN NYP" abbreviated "Ryan New York - Paris."

What is the moral of this story? Please think. Think, and think again.

CHAPTER ONE

CONSERVING NATURAL RESOURCES AND PROTECTING THE ENVIRONMENT, BECOMING AWARE OF OUR SURROUNDINGS AND SAVING THE EARTH, <u>AVOIDING/ PREVENTING WASTES</u>, POLLUTION AND GLOBAL WARMING THROUGH RECYCLING

This is for the attention of all parents and children, organizations and all nations on how to become aware of our surroundings and how we impact the earth, with special regards to AIR, LAND and WATER issues; and how to continue consciously and naturally to keep and preserve our beautiful earth through recycling and preservation; to ***prevent or reduce pollution and global warming.***

OUR WATER- For instance, about 78% of the water we use in the house is used in the bathroom and sometimes each of us uses more than 100 gallons every day.

ON OUR PART- Children and parents and everyone in your organization or nation need to know how to use low- flow water equipment, for example, shower heads, faucets, toilets; to save water and energy. Also, please contact your State Water Board for specific ways to not waste water.

OUR AIR- Trees and plants take in Carbon dioxide and produce needed Oxygen in cleaning our air. Millions of trees could be saved if people stopped receiving junk mail and the like.

ON OUR PART- In the USA, write to Mail Preference Service, Direct Marketing Association, 11 West 42nd Street, P. O. Box 3861, New York, NY 10163.

AIR- Likely areas of pollution are in the forms of smoke, odors, gases, bacteria, mildew, dust, mold, certain chemicals, animal dander, pollen and static electricity. These can pollute indoor air more readily than exhaust outdoors.

ON YOUR PART- Buy environmentally friendly cleaning products or choose natural alternatives such as baking soda or vinegar and water. Check and clean air filters and ventilation systems, vacuum your carpets regularly, wash and clean household utensils, and get your kids to do the same.

OUR LAND- In 1990, people spent more on food packaging than farmers received in net income. Packaging waste accounts for a third of all garbage sent to landfills. Recycling creates six times as many jobs as land does fill-up.

Pesticides and fertilizers are among the most deadly of chemicals. Over 270 billion pounds of artificial fertilizers are used on the earth each year. Artificial fertilizers deplete the Ozone layer and contribute to acid rain.

Nearly 80% of toxic wastes end in the ground. About 100 billion gallons of liquid hazardous wastes are absorbed into the ground water supplies every year from discarded waste ending up in 32million pounds of household cleaning products down the drain.

ON YOUR PART- Purchase organically grown and chemical free produce. Recycle motor oil. Dispose of paint, batteries and household chemicals correctly by contacting your local government or local County Health Department. Eliminate household solutions made from toxic petrochemicals.

The Three R's

Environmental problems wont just go away.

Parents, children, organizations, all nations and the entire community need to practice the three R's of environ- mentality: REDUCE, RE-USE and RECYCLE.

REDUCE- Many schools spend as much money disposing of their trash as they do buying textbooks. Americans discard enough office paper to build a 12- foot wall from Los Angeles to New York City yearly. Americans throw away enough aluminum to rebuild a commercial aircraft fleet every three months. Americans also use about 2 billion disposable razors every year!

ON YOUR PART- Don't buy over – packaged goods. Buy products in bulk. Cook from scratch. Opt for recyclable packaging and buy well- built goods, saving on repairs and replacement.

RE- USE- The creativity of our elders found new uses for many articles: Scraps of cloth became quilts and rugs, jars were reused each canning season, and rubber tires became swings. Go inside your offices and homes and re-use stuffs, please.

ON YOUR PART- Find new uses- paper becomes scratch pads; plastic milk jugs provide drip watering in gardens; lawn clippings become a natural mulch.

Reuse sandwich bags and aluminum foil. Use canvas shopping bags. Donate usable goods to schools or charities and shop at thrift and garage sales.

RECYCLE- Recycling just one aluminum will save enough energy to make 19 more! We improperly dispose of motor oil to repeat the Exxon Valdez oil spill every 2 ½ weeks. Paper products presently use about 35% of the world's annual timber harvest. But for every ton of paper made from wastepaper, we use half of the energy, half the water, produce 74% less air pollution, 35% less water pollution, save 17 pulp trees, reduce solid waste in our landfills and create five times as many jobs as the production of paper from virgin wood pulp.

ON YOUR PART- Know what materials can be recycled in your community. Purchase recycled products or those that can be recycled. Encourage expanded recycling processes. Also, you can help by not contaminating your recyclables with non-recyclable items.

But first, here are prerequisites:

1. Rinse empty bottles and cans. Dirty ones attract vermin.

2. Don't get carried away with rinsing water, especially hot water is a very precious commodity.

3. Peel cans, recycle the labels with your mixed paper.

4. Remove caps, stoppers and wire from the bottles.

5. Don't throw away your old teacup in with your bottles. The ceramic cup is made up of different materials and has a different melting point than the bottle glass. If the cup slips unnoticed

through the system, it can ruin a whole batch of glass.

6. Ditto light bulbs, glassware and window panes.

7. Paper soiled with food cannot be recycled. That means no dirty pizza boxes, no used paper plates, towels, napkins, no used Happy Meal boxes with ketchup on them.

8. Don't improvise. If you're not sure or wandering whether the recyclers will take Spot's metal water dish you just ran over, please call and enquire. If you want to recycle your old paperbacks that got rained on before goodwill

picks them up, call and ask. If you would like to throw in your aluminum teapot that melted last week, call and ask.

And never give up recycling. Please keep up the good work. Recycling is something that can make us all happy and healthy, which we could be proud of.

Identifying recyclables

1. Aluminum cans

2. Cardboard

3. Glass bottles and jars

4. Metals

5. Used motor oil

6. Grocery bags

7. Tin or steel cans

8. Magazines

9. Automobile batteries

10. Office papers

11. Clothing

12. Newspapers

13. Plastic bottles

14. Styrene "Styrofoam"

15. White goods, appliances

Unusual recyclables includes carpet pad, polyurethane and rebound, computers, concrete, asphalt, trees, industrial plastics, laser printer cartridges, phone books, plates and window glass, foam packing materials and textiles.

Sorting Glass for Recycling:

Acceptable:

(1) Soda bottles

(2) Wine and liquor bottles

(3)   Juice containers

(4)   Ketchup bottles

(5)   Food jars

(6)   Beer bottles

Not Acceptable:

(1)   Ceramic cups and plates

(2)   Clay flowers pots

(3)   Light bulbs

(4)   Window glass

(5)   Heat- resistant ovenware

(6) Drinking glasses

Resources:

(a) Colorado Office of Energy Conservation

(b) Colorado Recyclers (Recycling Guide)

(c) Air Quality Control/ Clean Air Colorado

(d) National Jewish Center for Immunology and Respiratory Medicine (information on air quality and health)

(e) Denver Water Board

(f) Ecosource Catalog

Recycling helps economic growth, the Colorado example among the many advantages of recycling is that the use of delectable natural resources can directly stimulate economic growth and can reduce capital investment diverted to environmental protection.

The Colorado State Government realized this when a bill was signed into law (HB1245) in 1991, by Governor Roy Romer. The law is to use tax incentives to promote recycling by encouraging manufacturers to use more recycled products as raw materials. The law is the first of its kind in the

USA. It grants an income tax credit to firms that buy equipment needed to make products from 25% or more recyclable scrap. And by encouraging the growth of these markets, we can help make recycling more cost effective.

All nations should please emulate the good example for encouraging recycling set by the State of Colorado.

Nature has given us so much, and since we cannot pay nature back, let us try to keep the earth natural though. Parents, please teach your children to plant trees frequently, and not to destroy plants or pollute the environment; and to please keep the environment clean, tidy and natural. We should not to only plants trees, but we should maintain our trees, grasses and our flowers. And finally, we should form a good habit toward nature. For instance, if we see broken bottles or sharp pins, etc, on the ground, we ought to be kind enough to pick them up and put them where they belong: in the dust bin of course! Parents, please always teach your children this lesson, to enable them to grow up and maintain a clean and tidy environment.

Engage your organizations or nations in green initiatives and environmentally friendly business practices that are sustainable in the future, please. Opt for solar energy, use less air conditioners or none at all, use wind power; figure out modern ways to build homes and offices with natural air coming in, and natural lights coming in through the roof or body of the home or offices, etc. ***Do everything humanly possible to curtain wastes or reduce wastes to zero and save lots of money in your business or in your country, and then have plenty of money in your savings account or lots of*** *fuel in your aero plane, like Charles Lindberg did in 1927, in your flight across the Atlantic to the future. I hope somebody is listening.*

Thank you!

Take good care of yourself, eat balanced diet, lots of fruits and vegetables, and drink water daily, exercise daily, please fall in love have good sex more frequently, keep good friends who are ready to be educated and work hard in life to earn enough money to enjoy their lives, be friendly with everyone regardless of race, gender, ethnicity, greed or religion, make everyone your friend and your family, give to the poor always, help the needy always, be the first to say hello to friends and strangers, be smart and stay away from trouble always, talk less, listen more, better yourself daily, improve your life daily, forgive always, respect and protect girls and women always, laugh daily and be around happy people, do humor, take life easy, enjoy life while it lasts, go out and get the millions of dollars waiting for you, since no one is born to be poor, get education and seek information daily, be rich in morality, do those things that are excellent, and have lots, and lots of fun! Bye!

This is Gabriel Atsepoyi, an American Soldier. He studied Law (LL.B), BA History, MBA and a Doctorate Degrees in Management. (Univ of Colorado, Cambridge, etc). **If you have special talent and you want sponsorship to the USA or any country, please get in touch with me pronto**. You can also consult me for Leadership ideas, and ways to improve any government or corporation. I **am ready and able to help the USA Government or Nigeria Government anytime. Please call me! 720 934 1983 USA.**

CONTACT ME ANYTIME: Gabriel.atsepoyi@yahoo.com Or gatsepoyi@gmail.com

Telephone number in the United States: 720 934 1983

Or write to me regarding any other business you wish to do with me, like Wealth Management, Partnerships, or any issue, etc. Send your letters to:

Gabriel B. Atsepoyi

Doctorate program

5775 DTC BLVD, SUITE 100

GREENWOOD VILLAGE, COLORADO 80111 USA

FAX 303 694 6673

THE BOOK OF TOTAL HAPPINESS
by Gabriel B. Atsepoyi (Akpieyi)

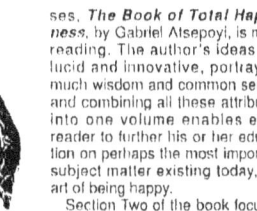

Education is the key to learning any subject better, so why should it be any different when it comes to being happy? This is the premise for Gabriel Atsepoyi's *The Book of Total Happiness*, in which the author gives new meaning to the search for happiness and contentment in one's life.

It has been said that psychological maturity is achieved when one gains a secure understanding of the meaning of life and one's place in it. This fascinating volume explores this matter in full detail concerning happiness, marriage, health and physical well being.

Regardless of religious or philosophical persuasion, readers will become engrossed in this presentation, which to its credit does not intend to talk down to readers, but instead provides working guidelines in a straightforward and easily understood fashion.

Given the high rate of divorce these days, Mr. Atsepoyi believes that without some form of education concerning marriage, the do's and don't's, the expectations and the compromises, people are destined to continue to allow this shocking statistic to grow. This book's goal, therefore, is to begin that education, to provide understandable paths toward that elusive spiritual habitat, being happy. It's not as easy as it seems, says the author, and most people have to work at it. Yet, it is not totally out of reach, if one can look at life with honest appraisal and work to change those things that hinder one's happiness.

One of the more intriguing aspects of this book is the point that not everyone achieves the same level of happiness, nor has the same avenues available to them in their search for personal happiness. That is fine, says the author, because no two people are exactly the same. Each must find that place that is comfortable for him or her, then work to maintain those good feelings through effort and commitment.

Mr. Atsepoyi's prose is fluid and expressive, and his observations are shrewdly punctuated by a basic wisdom that will appeal to all. But what makes this book be singled out from the many is the significant contribution it makes toward re-educating people of the how and why of being happy. This serves a most practical purpose, first in helping the reader to find paths and guidelines for being happy, the author is also boldly illustrating the power of individual expression, positive thinking, and having a goal to work toward.

Highly recommended for its insight and analyses, *The Book of Total Happiness*, by Gabriel Atsepoyi, is must reading. The author's ideas are lucid and innovative, portraying much wisdom and common sense, and combining all these attributes into one volume enables each reader to further his or her education on perhaps the most important subject matter existing today, the art of being happy.

Section Two of the book focuses on: A-Z about HIV/AIDS and the latest facts on AIDS, protection for kids and family, women's rights (the need to respect and protect women), smoking and its hazards, environmental protection/prevention, how and the need for better education for children, etc., etc.

THE BOOK OF TOTAL HAPPINESS
ABOUT THE AUTHOR

Gabriel Atsepoyi (Akpieyi), twenty-six years old, was born in Africa and presently resides in Colorado.

An avid reader, Mr. Atsepoyi makes it known that the only way he is happy is when he is helping others. His love of God serves his existence well, as he expands upon his belief that one's knowledge is one's power in leading a happy and successful life.

A member of the Optimist Club of Arvada, the author has had many articles published previously on a variety of topics, yet his overriding concerns are for the rate of divorce and its effects toward broken homes, unhappy families, neglected children, uneducated and uncultured children, and crime. He has propounded many solutions in these areas in his latest work, and his hope is that readers will reflect upon those suggestions.

THE BOOK OF TOTAL HAPPINESS
by Gabriel B. Atsepoyi (Akpieyi)

Education is the key to learning any subject better, so why should it be any different when it comes to being happy? This is the premise for Gabriel Atsepoyi's *The Book of Total Happiness*, in which the author gives new meaning to the search for happiness and contentment in one's life.

It has been said that psychological maturity is achieved when one gains a secure understanding of the meaning of life and one's place in it. This fascinating volume explores this matter in full detail concerning happiness, marriage, health and physical well-being. Regardless of religious or philosophical persuasion, readers will become engrossed in this presentation, which to its credit does not intend to talk down to readers, but instead provides working guidelines in a straightforward and easily understood fashion.

Given the high rate of divorce these days, Mr. Atsepoyi believes that without some form of education concerning marriage, the do's and don'ts, the expectations and the compromises, people are destined to continue to allow this shocking statistic to grow. This book's goal, therefore, is to begin that education, to provide understandable paths toward that elusive spiritual habitat, being happy. It's not as easy as it seems, says the author, and most people have to work at it, but it is not totally out of reach, if one can cooperate with honest appraisal and work to change those things that hinder one's happiness.

One of the more intriguing aspects of the book is the point that not everyone achieves the same level of happiness, nor has the same avenues available to them in their search for personal happiness. That is fine, says the author, because no two people are exactly the same. Each must fine that place that is comfortable for him or her, then work to maintain those good feelings through effort and commitment.

Mr. Atsepoyi's prose is fluid and expressive, and his observations are shrewdly punctuated by a basic wisdom that will appeal to all. But what makes this book be singled out from the many is the significant contribution it makes toward re-educating people of the how and why of being happy. This serves a most practical purpose, first in helping the reader to find paths and guidelines for being happy, the author is also boldly illustrating the power of individual expression, positive thinking, and having a goal to work toward.

Highly recommended for its insight and analyses, *The Book of Total Happiness*, by Gabriel Atsepoyi, is must reading. The author's ideas are lucid and innovative, portraying much wisdom and common sense, and combining all these attributes into one volume enables each reader to further his or her education on perhaps the most important subject matter existing today, the art of being happy.

Section Two of the book focuses on: A-Z about HIV/AIDS and the latest facts on AIDS, protection for kids and family, women's rights (the need to respect and protect women), smoking and its hazards, environmental protection/prevention, how and the need for better education for children, etc., etc.

THE BOOK OF TOTAL HAPPINESS
ABOUT THE AUTHOR

Gabriel Atsepoyi (Akpieyi), twenty-six years old, was born in Africa and presently resides in Colorado.

An avid reader, Mr. Atsepoyi makes it known that the only way he is happy is when he is helping others. His love of God serves his existence well as he expands upon his belief that one's knowledge of one's power in leading a happy and successful life.

A member of the Optimist Club of Arvada, the author has had many articles published previously on a variety of topics, yet his overriding concerns are for the rate of divorce and its effects toward broken homes, unhappy families, neglected children, uneducated and uncultured children, and crime. He has propounded many solutions in these areas in his latest work, and his hope is that readers will reflect upon those suggestions.

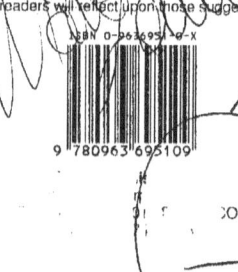

ISBN 0-9636951-8-X

HOW TO BE A GREAT MANAGER AND A GREAT LEADER BOTH AT THE WORK PLACE & AT HOME (PART 8)

PART EIGHT (NOTE: SO MANY SERIES COMING IN THE FUTURE)

By Prince Gabriel

Hon. Member US Army, MBA, Doctorate in Management

JD Candidate

Copyright ©Prince Gabriel 2010

INTRODUCTION

"I've missed more than 3,000
Shots in my career,
I've lost more than 300
Games,
26 times I've been trusted to
Take the game winning
Shot
And missed
I've failed over and over
Again in my life...
And that is why I succeed"

- Michael Jordan

Lincoln's "Failures"?

Below is one version of the so-called "Lincoln failures" list, shown in bold type. It's often used to inspire people to overcome life's difficulties with Lincoln as a model. Then look at the right column with other facts from Lincoln's pre-presidential life. History professor Lucas Morel compiled this comparison from the Chronology in *Selected Speeches and Writings/Lincoln* by Don E. Fehrenbacher, ed., 1992.

YEAR	FAILURES or SETBACKS	SUCCESSES
1832	**Lost job** **Defeated for state legislature**	Elected company captain of Illinois militia in Black Hawk War
1833	**Failed in business**	Appointed postmaster of New Salem, Illinois Appointed deputy surveyor of Sangamon County
1834		Elected to Illinois state legislature
1835	**Sweetheart died**	
1836	**Had nervous breakdown**	Re-elected to Illinois state legislature (running first in his district) Received license to practice law in Illinois state courts
1837		Led Whig delegation in moving Illinois state capital from Vandalia to Springfield Became law partner of John T. Stuart

1838	Defeated for Speaker	Nominated for Illinois House Speaker by Whig caucus Re-elected to Illinois House (running first in his district) Served as Whig floor leader
1839		Chosen presidential elector by first Whig convention Admitted to practice law in U.S. Circuit Court
1840		Argues first case before Illinois Supreme Court Re-elected to Illinois state legislature
1841		Established new law practice with Stephen T. Logan
1842		Admitted to practice law in U.S. District Court
1843	**Defeated for nomination for Congress**	
1844		Established own law practice with William H. Herndon as junior partner
1846		Elected to Congress
1848	**Lost renomination**	(Chose not to run for Congress, abiding by rule of rotation among Whigs.)
1849	**Rejected for land officer**	Admitted to practice law in U.S. Supreme Court Declined appointment as secretary and then as governor of Oregon Territory
1854	**Defeated for U.S. Senate**	Elected to Illinois state legislature (but declined seat to run for U.S. Senate)
1856	**Defeated for nomination for Vice President**	
1858	**Again defeated for U.S. Senate**	

1860		Elected President

My Failures: While in Basic training in the United States Army, several years ago, I had to qualify in the shooting range. That is where you aim at a target that pops up from the ground or from unknown places; I was expected to kill my target within seconds before my target vanishes. If you cannot aim and shoot quickly and accurately here you are not qualified to be an American Soldier, period.

I had never owned a gun in my life. I never even had a toy gun. I grew up in the village of Africa, in a small village called Ugborodo, or "Escravos", blessed with lots of crude oil (Chevron USA and others are exploiting our crude with virtually nothing of value for the people in my village!).

Here I was with a loaded gun, trying very hard to shoot down my enemies without luck. It was like telling a new born baby who does not understand any language yet to go and cook a delicious food! That would be impossible, wouldn't it? I was given several chances to qualify, but to no avail.

So, I was given an extra time, after exhausting all the times normally required. There were three other ladies with me who had not qualified; but quickly qualified. The time was about 6.30pm. The entire Soldiers in the Battalion were waiting patiently for me to do something magical to qualify. I had been trying to qualify for more than a week; shooting and wasting ammunitions for about twelve hours daily, but to no avail.

This last hour was my hour. The soldiers were hungry. It was 6.30pm. By 7pm, it would be too dark to continue the exercise. Solders were famished. The next day was graduation from Basic Training. All the male soldiers had qualified, except for me, an African boy from an obscure place called Ugborodo Village, "Escravos", in West Africa. What should I do?

I decided to lie down to relax. I was facing up. I looked into the sky. I relaxed my nerves. I meditated for about ten minutes. As I closed my eyes, I quickly slept off. I was very tired. I was snoring very loudly. During the ten minutes of nap everything in my body got refreshed. It was a reset of some sort. It was probably the best ten minutes of rest time I had ever had in my whole life! The Captain of the Battalion walked to me and gently pushed on me "wake up...let's do it!", as he whispered those courageous words into my ears.

I got up, took my M16, positioned my body right, breathed in and out softly, aimed and fired. The first twenty-four targets that popped up, I shot all down! I immediately became a sharp shooter! The Captain called off the training. It was about 6:55pm. The rest is history.

Now, how many leadership lessons can you see here? Think.

CHAPTER ONE

FROM FAILURES COME SUCCESS

As you can see from all the stories or testimonies above, there are disappointments and failures in life. As a manager, leader or parent, or as a person striving to make it to the top, you are going to encounter a lot of failures. Don't be afraid to fail. Try it again. Improve every time. For, doing nothing is not an option.

Take a cue from Abraham Lincoln, try something different. Go into a different profession. Especially at a time of economic recession: go back to the university or to a technical training place and get more training, or more advanced degrees or skills. Get more information. Get help from people with experiences. Ask questions. Prepare yourself well and accomplish your goals in spite of your failures in the past. Just persevere a little bit more and you will succeed. I guarantee it!

Reinvent yourself: if you truly want to be a great manager, leader or person, for goodness sake know how to reinvent yourself; and please do it very quickly, if you must survive and thrive today. The competition for jobs, promotions, for higher offices or for executive positions are done in a fiercely, very competitive ways. The more education, skill trainings, years of experiences, and of course, connections, and likeable attitudes, the better you can reinvent yourself, and leave a troubling profession to another one with ease. Please move fast, be careful, be prudent, but act fast! **<u>Do not procrastinate in anything in life</u>. <u>Move forward, move fast. So, reinvent</u>**

yourself, my friend! Go and get other skills or training in a more rewarding profession, or a technical training in high demand areas like in the healthcare profession, nursing, medical doctor, healthcare management, pharmacy, or in engineering, and so on, and stop complaining and whining about everything! Be diligent and get some goodluck, ok!

God bless you!

CHAPTER TWO

WHAT IS IN THERE FOR ME?

While I was struggling to qualify in the United States Army, I quickly, quietly thought to myself "what is in there for me?"

Then, I realized if I did not qualify I would not be given the $10,000 sign-in bonus for new soldiers. I would not get an 'honorable discharge', one of the highest honors in the United States Army. My college loans, then, more than $60,000 would not be paid by the US Army. I would find it very difficult to get anything of value from the American society, if disqualified from the US Army.

However, if I qualify, all my university loans will be paid, I will get more than $10,000 in my bank account, and my future education and doctorate programs will be paid, and if I am injured in the service I will be paid compensations and pensions for the rest of my life, my wife and children will receive salaries for the rest of their lives...The benefits for success in the United States Army are just too much for me to fail!

Now, what tangible things or things of value can you come up with to convince all your employees or people in your country to come on board with you and support you and help you to accomplish all your goals? Please be honest. Great leaders MUST keep their word or promise, ok. What is in there for others for them to support and help you out? Remember: life is about *"quid pro quo"* or 'give and take'. Be fair. Be just. Be conscientious. Do equity. Just be nice to others ok.

CHAPTER THREE

Do you have ideas? Can you come up with cool, new ideas? Do you have innovative, break-through ideas? Can you be creative with your unique ideas? As a great manager/leader or great person can you keep thinking all day and night for innovative ideas? And if you have innovative ideas can you put them into ACTIONS for the benefit of society? Do it now. Please. Thanks!

Take good care of yourself, eat balanced diet, lots of fruits and vegetables, and drink water daily, exercise daily, please fall in love have good sex more frequently, keep good friends who are ready to be educated and work hard in life to earn enough money to enjoy their lives, be friendly with everyone regardless of race, gender, ethnicity, greed or religion, make everyone your friend and your family, give to the poor always, help the needy always, be the first to say hello to friends and strangers, be smart and stay away from trouble always, talk less, listen more, better yourself daily, improve your life daily, forgive always, respect and protect girls and women always, laugh daily and be around happy people, do humor, take life easy, enjoy life while it lasts, go out and get the millions of dollars waiting for you, since no one is born to be poor, get education and seek information daily, be rich in morality, do those things that are excellent, and have lots, and lots of fun! Bye!

Intentionally left blank

Intentionally left blank

This is Gabriel Atsepoyi, an American Soldier. He studied Law (LL.B), BA History, MBA and a Doctorate Degrees in Management. (Univ of Colorado, Cambridge, etc). **If you have special talent and you want sponsorship to the USA or any country, please get in touch with me pronto**. You can also consult me for Leadership ideas, and ways to improve any government or corporation. I **am ready and able to help the USA Government or Nigeria Government anytime. Please call me! 720 934 1983 USA.**

CONTACT ME ANYTIME: Gabriel.atsepoyi@yahoo.com Or gatsepoyi@gmail.com

Telephone number in the United States: 720 934 1983

Or write to me regarding any other business you wish to do with me, like Wealth Management, Partnerships, or any issue, etc. Send your letters to:

Gabriel B. Atsepoyi

Doctorate program

5775 DTC BLVD, SUITE 100

GREENWOOD VILLAGE, COLORADO 80111 USA

FAX 303 694 6673

THE BOOK OF TOTAL HAPPINESS
by Gabriel B. Atsepoyi (Akpieyi)

Education is the key to learning any subject better, so why should it be any different when it comes to being happy? This is the premise for Gabriel Atsepoyi's *The Book of Total Happiness*, in which the author gives new meaning to the search for happiness and contentment in one's life.

It has been said that psychological maturity is achieved when one gains a secure understanding of the meaning of life and one's place in it. This fascinating volume explores this matter in full detail concerning happiness, marriage, health and physical well being.

Regardless of religious or philosophical persuasion, readers will become engrossed in this presentation, which to its credit does not intend to talk down to readers, but instead provides working guidelines in a straightforward and easily understood fashion.

Given the high rate of divorce these days, Mr. Atsepoyi believes that without some form of education concerning marriage, the do's and don'ts, the expectations and the compromises, people are destined to continue to allow this shocking statistic to grow. This book's goal, therefore, is to begin that education, to provide understandable paths toward that elusive spiritual habitat, being happy. It's not as easy as it seems, says the author, and most people have to work at it. Yet, it is not totally out of reach, if one can look at life with honest appraisal and work to change those things that hinder one's happiness.

One of the more intriguing aspects of this book is the point that not everyone achieves the same level of happiness, nor has the same avenues available to them in their search for personal happiness. That is fine, says the author, because no two people are exactly the same. Each must find that place that is comfortable for him or her, then work to maintain those good feelings through effort and commitment.

Mr. Atsepoyi's prose is fluid and expressive, and his observations are shrewdly punctuated by a basic wisdom that will appeal to all. But what makes this book be singled out from the many is the significant contribution it makes toward re-educating people of the how and why of being happy. This serves a most practical purpose, first in helping the reader to find paths and guidelines for being happy, the author is also boldly illustrating the power of individual expression, positive thinking, and having a goal to work toward.

Highly recommended for its insight and analyses, *The Book of Total Happiness*, by Gabriel Atsepoyi, is must reading. The author's ideas are lucid and innovative, portraying much wisdom and common sense, and combining all these attributes into one volume enables each reader to further his or her education on perhaps the most important subject matter existing today, the art of being happy.

Section Two of the book focuses on: A-Z about HIV/AIDS and the latest facts on AIDS, protection for kids and family, women's rights (the need to respect and protect women), smoking and its hazards, environmental protection/prevention, how and the need for better education for children, etc., etc.

THE BOOK OF TOTAL HAPPINESS

ABOUT THE AUTHOR

Gabriel Atsepoyi (Akpieyi), twenty-six years old, was born in Africa and presently resides in Colorado.

An avid reader, Mr. Atsepoyi makes it known that the only way he is happy is when he is helping others. His love of God serves his existence well, as he expands upon his belief that one's knowledge is one's power in leading a happy and successful life.

A member of the Optimist Club of Arvada, the author has had many articles published previously on a variety of topics, yet his overriding concerns are for the rate of divorce and its effects toward broken homes, unhappy families, neglected children, uneducated and uncultured children, and crime. He has propounded many solutions in these areas in his latest work, and his hope is that readers will reflect upon those suggestions.

THE BOOK OF TOTAL HAPPINESS
by Gabriel B. Atsepoyi (Akpieyi)

Education is the key to learning any subject better, so why should it be any different when it comes to being happy? This is the premise for Gabriel Atsepoyi's *The Book of Total Happiness*, in which the author gives new meaning to the search for happiness and contentment in one's life.

It has been said that psychological maturity is achieved when one gains a secure understanding of the meaning of life and one's place in it. This fascinating volume explores this matter in full detail concerning happiness, marriage, health and physical well-being. Regardless of religious or philosophical persuasion, readers will become engrossed in this presentation, which to its credit does not intend to talk down to readers, but instead provides working guidelines in a straightforward and easily understood fashion.

Given the high rate of divorce these days, Mr. Atsepoyi believes that without some form of education concerning marriage, the do's and don't's, the expectations and the compromises, people are destined to continue to allow this shocking statistic to grow. This book's goal, therefore, is to begin that education, to provide understandable paths toward that elusive spiritual habitat, being happy. It's not as easy as it seems, says the author, and most people have to work at it. It is not totally out of reach, if one can look at life with honest appraisal and work to change those things that hinder one's happiness.

One of the more intriguing aspects of the book is the point that not everyone achieves the same level of happiness, nor has the same avenues available to them in their search for personal happiness. That is fine, says the author, because no two people are exactly the same. Each must fine that place that is comfortable for him or her, then work to maintain those good feelings through effort and commitment.

Mr. Atsepoyi's prose is fluid and expressive, and his observations are shrewdly punctuated by a basic wisdom that will appeal to all. But what makes this book be singled out from the many is the significant contribution it makes toward re-educating people of the how and why of being happy. This serves a most practical purpose, first in helping the reader to find paths and guidelines for being happy, the author is also boldly illustrating the power of individual expression, positive thinking, and having a goal to work toward.

Highly recommended for its insight and analyses, *The Book of Total Happiness*, by Gabriel Atsepoyi, is must reading. The author's ideas are lucid and innovative, portraying much wisdom and common sense, and combining all these attributes into one volume enables each reader to further his or her education on perhaps the most important subject matter existing today, the art of being happy.

Section Two of the book focuses on: A-Z about HIV/AIDS and the latest facts on AIDS, protection for kids and family, women's rights (the need to respect and protect women), smoking and its hazards, environmental protection/prevention, how and the need for better education for children, etc., etc.

THE BOOK OF TOTAL HAPPINESS

ABOUT THE AUTHOR

Gabriel Atsepoyi (Akpieyi), twenty-six years old, was born in Africa and presently resides in Colorado.

An avid reader, Mr. Atsepoyi makes it known that the only way he is happy is when he is helping others. His love of God serves his existence well. He expands upon his belief that one's knowledge is one's power in leading a happy and successful life.

A member of the Optimist Club of Arvada, the author has had many articles published previously on a variety of topics, yet his overriding concerns are for the rate of divorce and its effects toward broken homes, unhappy families, neglected children, uneducated and uncultured children, and crime. He has propounded many solutions in these areas in his latest work, and his hope is that readers will reflect upon those suggestions.

ISBN 0-9636954-0-X

9 780963 695109

HOW TO BE A GREAT MANAGER AND A GREAT LEADER BOTH AT THE WORK PLACE & AT HOME (PART 9)

PART NINE (NOTE: SO MANY SERIES COMING IN THE FUTURE)

By Prince Gabriel

Hon. Member US Army, MBA, Doctorate in Management

JD Candidate

Copyright ©Prince Gabriel 2010

INTRODUCTION

When was the last time you swept your home thoroughly? When was the last time you went through every item of things you actually possessed? When was the last time you rearranged the position of your bed(s), chairs, tables, everything in your home or office? When was the last time you went through all your past and present mails, notes, letters, emails, messages? Are you keeping your receipts? All my receipts in the Western World for the past twenty years are intact! Do you keep receipts? Did you know you can turn your trashes or hidden resources into treasures? Now, how many of your resources or treasures have you preserved for future generations?

My wife recently went through my letters and discovered a check for $500 free of charge from a credit card company wanting me to try its platinum card for six months without any obligation to sign any contract. Yes, $500, in free money! The other day my wife found about $95 inside the pocket of my old jacket! My mother passed away at 73 years old, unknown to us the children, she had so many properties, lands, and cash starched away for her children, both born and unborn! Can you believe how much money is hiding or hidden in your junk mails or junk yards or in your organization or nation that is yet to be discovered? When you discover these treasures and money or natural resources, could you please preserve some, keep some locked away in a safe place (and pass laws to preserve them) for future generations. Please!

Every human being is capable of doing so many great things: like being a great musician, physicist, lawyer, and so on. Now, if you have so many people as employees in your organization or citizens of your country, can you please ginger them up, or do something to motivate them or help them to make full use of their potentials, raw talents and/or natural resources? Please.

In some countries like Saudi Arabia, Libya, Nigeria, Russia, and so on, with crude oil and so many other natural resources, yet when you go to these countries with crude oil, that is all these countries are focused on surviving, amidst several other resources that are left to waste away. The people in crude oil producing countries are not being given quality education and variety of skills to survive in the future in a global market when the oil dries up. As will see later in this paper, crude oil and other natural resources are drying up fast. What is going to happen to the once rich oil-countries like Nigeria and Saudi Arabia when crude oil dries up in the future? What is the future like for some organizations and nations of the world? Are you all going through your talents and natural resources to explore or find the hidden wealth, treasures and great stuffs hidden in your yards or homes or organization or nation and diversify your investments now and in the future before it is too late? Well, time will tell.

Now, can you serve people, let say, in a restaurant or in a bar? Can you smile, show happiness while serving the poor and the rich alike? Can you go down and wash off the dirt in somebody's feet? How humble can you be, managers and leaders?

Did you know that in order to be a great manager and a great leader, you have to first become like a little child? Can you be modest like a little child? Can you be innocent like a little child? There are a lot of excellent traits associated with little children that makes everyone love them and want to be with them, play with them and help them out at all times. Could you please find a little infant and stay with that little infant for a while, helping him/her in every way possible. At the end of that exercise, write down as many things as possible that you think would help you to become that great manager, leader or person that you desire to be. Good luck!

How many leadership lessons can you learn from the introduction above? Think.

CHAPTER ONE

MANAGERS AND LEADERS PROVIDE UNITY & STABILITY

A great manager/leader is usually very calm, speaks slowly, but forcefully. She brings everybody together; for out of many comes strength and unity. She brings stability by creating an atmosphere of natural affection, care and humane treatment for all and sundry; just like a real mother would treat her biological children. She is in charge, gives clear direction and delegates authority to everyone. And when something is wrong she takes responsibility for it. She talks quietly with that person.

A female manager/leader knows all the hidden spots, where treasures and wealth are being kept or forgotten at home, in the organization, or in your nation. The male leaders are equally good at finding hidden treasures. However, the female leaders have natural instincts that work perfectly almost all the times. We all have mothers or wives at some point and we all can relate in some way to this fact, can't we?

Preserving something for posterity/future: again, it is my proposition here to engage our female managers/leaders **equally**, just like our male leaders, in preserving our natural resources and/or hidden treasures for future generations. Our mothers are better suited naturally in preserving good things for their children unborn, aren't they?

Our crude oil and other natural resources are being depleted faster than we can ever replace them. Please let us invest heavily in quality education, science and technology.

I am calling on the great managers and great leaders in Nigeria and all oil producing countries and all nations of the world, for that matter, to invest more in quality education, science and technology now. I am referring to the same kind of education in Japan, Germany, China, United States and other industrialized nations of the world. I am begging the leaders of Nigeria to do everything humanly possible to adopt the system of education in the industrialized nations of the world today and help all Nigerians to have quality education, by giving them scholarships, loans, etc. Please. Time is running out. Please. Nigerian leaders, please unite the people of Nigeria, make almost all the languages in Nigeria official languages (please make Hausa, Ibo, Edo, Yoruba, Ijaw or Izon, Urhobo, Itsekiri, Ishan, and all these great languages to be Nigeria official languages, just like in South Africa!), cherish our cultures and traditions and repair all the roads in Nigeria (you can ask the Nigerian Army engineers to please supervise convicted inmates in jails or prisons eating free foods and others to repair our roads for little pay), do a complete overhaul of the Nigeria Prison Systems and investigate every prisoner in jail or prison who are innocent (and trust me there are so many innocent people in Nigeria Prisons or jails), free the innocent people in Nigeria jails/prisons with compensations, and get other convicted prisoners to help build new schools, roads, work in both private and government farms, and be paid for their work (in some places in the United States part of inmate salaries are given to the victims or people they hurt, part to the government, the rest is given to the inmates/prisoners or kept in a bank for them to start new life upon their release from prisons), build new schools, colleges and universities, establish big productive farms for all universities with Agricultural Department and let them produce enough foods to feed all Nigerians (just like you have in Brazil), challenge all engineering schools in Nigeria to produce cars and vehicles for Nigerians and for exports (and please fund these engineering schools well and get honest Nigerians to supervise how the funds are used prudently without being stolen), establish industries to preserve these foods and/or can agricultural products for export to China, Europe and other places, seriously curtail import of anything from China, Europe and the United States, let every Nigerian enroll in the University, regardless of whether or not they can pass the entrance examination to that university, and then coach that person to earn a good skill(s) according to his/her natural talents, abilities, etc. Electricity is free from the sun, wind, and other natural sources, my dear Nigerians! Please provide electricity to all Nigerians. Please!

Again, my dear Nigerians: the way forward is education, education, education. Quality education for all Nigerians ought to be implemented by the great leaders in Nigeria immediately without delay. Please. God bless you all!

CHAPTER TWO

OIL DEPLETION, INVEST IN YOUR FUTURE NOW OR ELSE...

Below is solid evidence about our crude oil and other natural resources being depleted fast and the dangers ahead for oil producing countries that delay in investing the oil money in education for all its' people, in science and technology, etc.

ENJOY IT!

Presentation at the Technical University of Clausthal

C.J.Campbell
December 2000

1. Title
Ladies and Gentlemen
· Thank you for inviting me to make this presentation.
· To-day, I am going to talk about the depletion of oil. I am a petroleum geologist and have been studying the subject directly and indirectly for many years. It is a very important subject, as is amply confirmed by recent events.
· I compliment the organisers for raising the subject in Germany. It is a large and strong country, which can exert its influence both on Europe and the World. Truth has always proved a powerful weapon. It needs to take action.

2. Sub-Title
The title of my talk is Peak Oil. It truly is a turning point for Mankind. It will affect us all. It is a large subject, and it will take us about an hour to work through it.

3. Purpose
The purpose of the talk is to evaluate the resource base and its depletion. Then we can go on to study the present crisis and try to see how it will evolve. Finally we can think specifically about Germany's predicament.

4. Main Points
In summary, these are the main points that we have to grasp:

- Conventional oil - and I will explain what I mean by that - provides most of the oil produced today, and is responsible for about 95% all oil that has been produced so far.
- It will continue to dominate supply for a long time to come. It is what matters most.
- Its discovery peaked in the 1960s. We now find one barrel for every four we consume.
- Middle East share of production is set to rise. The rest of the world peaked in 1997, and is therefore in terminal decline
- World peak comes within about five years
- Non-conventional oil delays peak only a few years, but will ameliorate the subsequent decline
- Gas, which is less depleted than oil, will likely peak around 2020

5. Discontinuity

- As I said, peak oil is a turning point for Mankind.
- The economic prosperity of the 20th Century was driven by cheap, oil-based energy
- Everyone had the equivalent of several unpaid and unfed slaves to do his work for him
- These slaves are now getting old and wont work much longer
- We need to find how to live without them

6 Slaves

The energy slaves of modern Man

7. Not a Repeat
I should stress that we are not facing a re-run of the Oil Shocks of the 1970s
· They were like the tremors that herald an earthquake, although serious enough, tipping the World into recession
· Now we face the earthquake itself
· This shock is very different. It is driven by resource constraints, not politics - although of course politics do enter into it.
· It is not a temporary interruption but the onset of a permanent new condition
· The warning signals have been flying for a long time. They have been plain to see. But the world turned a blind eye, and failed to read the message

8 Amazingly unprepared
· Our lack of preparedness is itself amazing, given the importance of oil

to our lives
· The warnings were rejected and discredited as if they were words of soothsayers and prophets.
· I myself have been called a Cassandra
· But the warnings were not prophecy
· It simply recognised two undeniable facts
· First: you have to find oil before you can produce it
· Second: production has to mirror discovery
· Discovery reached a peak in the 1960s - despite all the technology we hear so much about and a worldwide search for the best prospects
· It should surprise no one that we now face the corresponding peak of production. This simple reasoning has been however rejected by flat-earth economists and others with a blind faith in technology and markets forces. Worse still, governments have listened to bad advice.
· There are many vested interests bent on confusion and denial, which I will touch on later

9 Europe's Revolt
Let is look briefly at what happened in Europe a few weeks ago.
· The French fishermen blockaded the Channel Ports because their fuel costs had doubled, even though their fuel was already tax-free
· The dispute spread rapidly to England and other countries
· Schools were closed. Hospitals had a red alert
· Supermarkets started rationing bread
· Trade and industry was seriously interrupted: the cost was huge
· People lost confidence in their government : its popularity fell sharply
· If an interruption in supply lasting only a few days could cause such havoc, it surely demonstrates how utterly dependent on oil we have become.

10. Depletion
Depletion is an easy concept to grasp.

- Think of an Irish pub full of happy people. Think of their pleasure at the first sip from a full glass
- Think of the frowns that begin to cross their faces when their glasses are half-empty. They know they have drunk more than is left. It is the turning point
- Watch them savour the last drops
- But the evening is young. When the glasses are empty, they can order another round.
- But eventually closing time comes when there are no more rounds to be had
- That is the meaning of depletion
- We need to know how big each glass - or oilfield - is, and
- We need to know how many more rounds there are - that is to say how many more oilfields are left to find

11. Date of Peak

I stress that we are not about to run out of oil, but production is about to reach a peak. When peak comes depends on the issue of Rates
- Discovery Rate - we now find one barrel of conventional oil for every four we consume
- Extraction Rate is controlled by the physics of the reservoir
- Demand is driven by economic growth and price.

Remember price is not the same as cost. It depends on cost but also tax and scarcity

12. What to Measure

Before measuring something, the first step is to decide what exactly to measure. It is a question every butcher asks. Does he weigh the meat or the bones as well?
- There are many different kinds of oil
- Each has its own endowment in Nature, characteristics, costs, and rate of extraction.

· Production of each type starts and ends at zero reaching a peak in between,
· Some rise to peak slowly, others quickly
· We need to identify and measure each type : we need to separate the meat from the bones

13 Conventional Oil

It is convenient to identify so-called Conventional Oil. It is the meat not the bones. It has contributed most oil to-date and will dominate all supply long into the future. We may concentrate on it, as it controls the date of peak.
But there is no universal agreement on how to define it. Here I will exclude
· Oil from coal and "shale"
· Bitumen and Extra-Heavy Oil
· Heavy Oil
· Deepwater Oil
· Polar Oil
Natural Gas liquids are also excluded because they belong to the gas domain.
The database is not up to clearly distinguishing all these categories but we should at least know what we aim to do.

14. Simple Questions

We may start by asking two simple questions
· How much oil has been found? and
· When was it found?
They sound simple, but they are difficult to answer because the data are weak.

15. Ambiguity & Bad Data

There is no consistency in what is reported.

· There is a large range even for production, which is simply reading the meter
· Reserve estimates are still less reliable
· The treatment of gas liquids ranges widely

There are two main sources of public data.
· The Oil & Gas Journal and World Oil are trade journals that compile information given to them by governments. They are not qualified to assess the validity of the information.
· Another widely used source is the BP Statistical Review. BP is in a position to evaluate the data, but it declines to do so, and instead just reproduces the Oil and Gas Journal.
· Lastly is the industry database, which is relatively reliable but too expensive for most analysts to access.
· All these sources are different. None of them are very intelligently compiled.

16 Reserve Reporting
· The industry has systematically under-reported the size of discovery for a host of good commercial and regulatory reasons. It understandably prefers to revise the reserves upwards over time than book them all up front. It is not its job to forecast the future.
· For most purposes, it does not matter, but we need to know the real record of the past if we are to use the trend to forecast the future.
· Governments variously under-report or over-report, or simply fail to update their estimates. As many as 70 countries reported unchanged numbers in 1999, which is utterly implausible.
· We need the "best estimate". It is often called Proved & Probable, such that any revisions are statistically neutral

17 Dating Revisions
· An oilfield contains what it contains because it was filled in the geological past, but knowledge of how much it contains evolves over

time.
· If we want a genuine discovery trend, we need to backdate revisions to the discovery of the field.
· Failure to backdate gives the illusion that more is being found than is the case. It is a cause of great misunderstanding

18 BP Reserves

This demonstrates how BP reports reserves, failing to backdate the revisions. It has misled many analysts. The large increases in the late 1980s were simply due to the OPEC quota wars. Nothing was actually added, as I will explain.

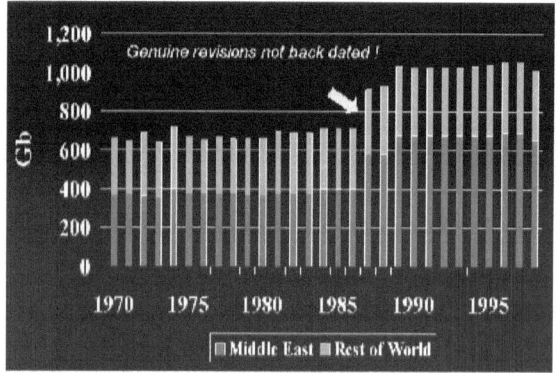

19 Spurious Revisions

I should explain this large increase in greater detail.
· Kuwait added 50% in 1985 to increase its OPEC quota, which was based partly on reserves. No corresponding new discoveries had been made. Nothing particular changed in the reservoir.
· Venezuela doubled its reserves in 1987 by the inclusion of large deposits of heavy oil that had been known for years.

· It forced the other OPEC countries to retaliate with huge increases
· Note too how the numbers have changed little since despite production..

But it is not quite as simple as that, because the early numbers were too low, having been inherited from the companies before they were expropriated. Some of the increase was justified but it has to be backdated to the discovery of the fields concerned that had been found up to 50 years before.

Year	Abu Dhabi	Dubai	Iran	Iraq	Kuwait	Neutral Zone	Saudi Arabia	Venezuela
1980	28.0	1.4	58.0	31.0	65.4	6.1	163.4	17.9
1981	29.0	1.4	57.5	30.0	65.9	6.0	165.0	18.0
1982	30.6	1.3	57.0	29.7	64.5	5.9	164.6	20.3
1983	30.5	1.4	55.3	41.0	64.2	5.7	162.4	21.5
1984	30.4	1.4	51.0	43.0	63.9	5.6	166.0	24.9
1985	30.5	1.4	48.5	44.5	90.0	5.4	169.0	25.9
1986	30.0	1.4	47.9	44.1	89.8	5.4	168.8	25.6
1987	31.0	1.4	48.8	47.1	91.9	5.3	166.6	25.0
1988	92.2	4.0	92.9	100.0	91.9	5.2	167.0	56.3
1989	92.2	4.0	92.9	100.0	91.9	5.2	170.0	58.1
1990	92.2	4.0	92.9	100.0	91.9	5.0	257.5	59.1
1991	92.2	4.0	92.9	100.0	94.5	5.0	257.5	59.1
1992	92.2	4.0	92.9	100.0	94.0	5.0	257.9	62.7
1993	92.2	4.0	92.9	100.0	94.0	5.0	258.7	63.3
1994	92.2	4.3	89.3	100.0	94.0	5.0	258.7	64.5
1995	92.2	4.3	88.2	100.0	94.0	5.0	258.7	64.9
1996	92.2	4.0	93.0	112.0	94.0	5.0	259.0	64.9
1997	92.2	4.0	93.0	112.5	94.0	5.0	259.0	71.7
1998	92.2	4.0	89.7	112.5	94.0	5.0	259.0	72.6
1999	92.2	4.0	89.7	112.5	94.0	5.0	261.0	72.6

20 Popular Image

The failure to backdate gives this misleading popular image of growing reserves. It is widely used by flat-earth economists in support of classical economic theories of supply and demand

I hasten to add that by no means all economists believe in a flat-earth. There are enlightened economists who now relate economics with resources, and they are coming to the fore.

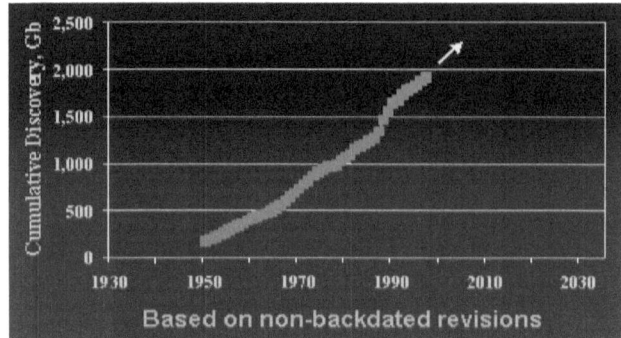

21 Reality & Illusion

This shows the effect of proper backdating. The discovery trend shown in yellow is falling not rising.

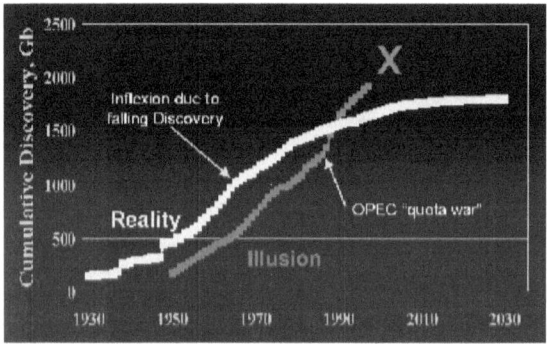

22 Impact of Technology

You will hear many claims for technology. No one disputes the huge technological advances of the industry. But, what has been the impact?
· In Exploration, it shows better both where oil is and where it is NOT - thus allowing better estimates of the potential to be made.
· In Production, it keeps production rate higher for longer, but has little impact on the reserves themselves
Note that much of the oil in a reservoir cannot be extracted because it

is held there by capillary forces and natural constrictions. The percentage recovered can be improved in some cases by injecting steam and such methods, but by no means all fields are susceptible to treatment. Most modern fields are produced to maximum efficiency from the outset.

23 Prudhoe Bay
This is well illustrated by the Prudhoe Bay field. It is the largest field in N. America.
· The Operator internally estimated its reserves at 12.5 Gb in 1977, but reported 9 Gb.
· Various enhanced recovery methods were started in 1982
· Decline commenced in 1988. Enhanced recovery did arrest decline for one year, but then the decline was steeper.
· The field will barely make the original estimate. Nothing was added This is quite typical. I could show you may similar examples.
Such plots are incidentally a good way to estimate genuine reserves

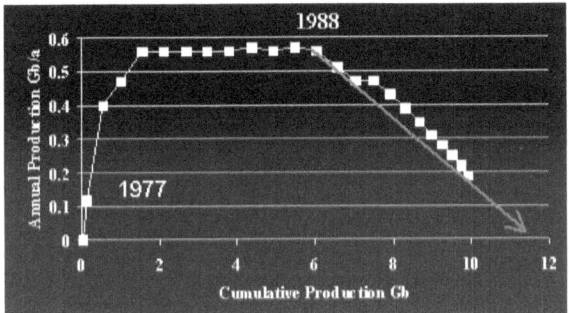

24. Yet-to-Find
Now let's turn to how much is yet-to-find

25 North Sea Generation
· A geochemical breakthrough in the 1980s made it possible to relate

the oil in a well with the rock from which it came.
· It became possible to identify and map the generating belts. They are few and far between because prolific oil was formed only under very rare geological circumstances. In fact, most of it comes from no more that three or four epochs of intense global warming
· This shows where the oil comes from in the North Sea. It was formed about 145 million years ago at the end of the Jurassic period.
· There is no possibility of finding oil outside these generating trends, and we now know where most of them are.

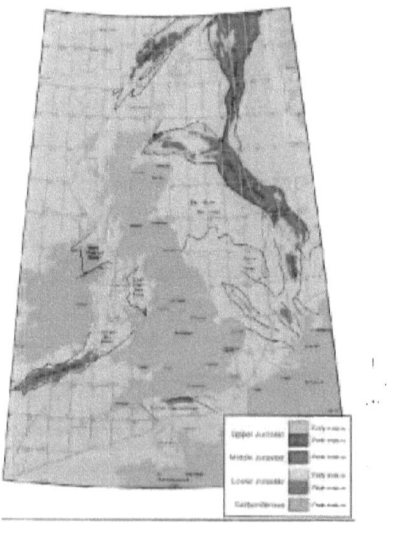

26 Seismic
Great advances in seismic technology make it possible to see the smallest and most subtle trap.
· In general, this better knowledge has reduced the perceived potential, because it shows the absence of large prospects.
· We can find a needle in a haystack, but it is still a needle. We did not need the resolution to find the giant fields holding most of the world's

oil.
· It means we have a much better knowledge of the endowment in Nature than we used to have.

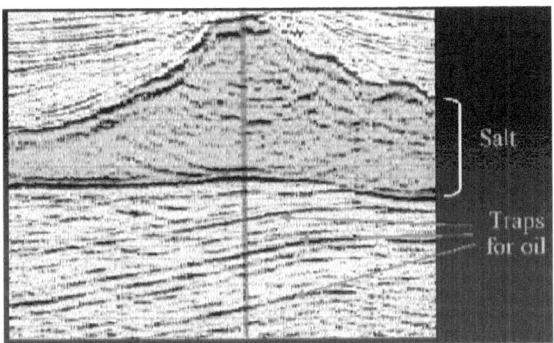

27 Creaming Curve

This is the so-called creaming curve.
· It plots discovery against exploration wildcats. They are the wells that either do - or do not - find a new field
· The largest fields are usually found first for obvious reasons, being too large to miss.
· The curve flattens until new discoveries are too small to be viable. It gives a good idea of how much is left to find.
· There are other statistical techniques but there is n't time to cover them here

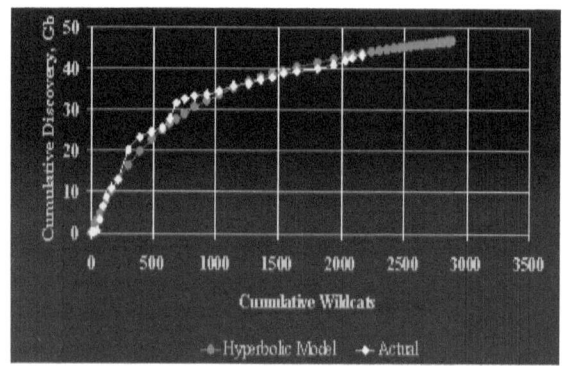

28 Shell Experience
· The same applies to an individual oil company
· Shell has found about 60 Gb with almost 4000 exploration wells, drilled over its entire history since 1895. If it drilled as many again, it could expect to find only 16 Gb
· Other companies have not had such a successful record.

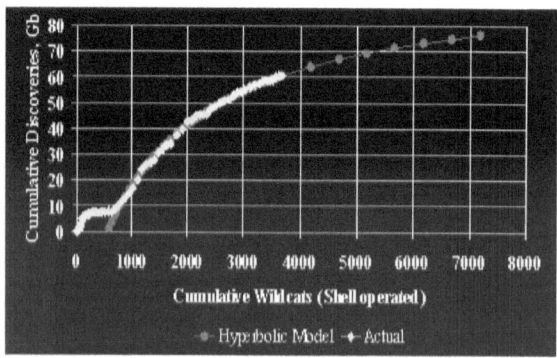

29 Parameters
To sum up, these are the main parameters for conventional oil.
· The numbers are shown as computed but should be generously rounded
· We have produced almost half what is there, and we have found

about 90%
· We produce 22 Gb a year but find only 6 Gb. That is to say, we find one for every four we consume from our inheritance of past discovery
· The current depletion rate is about 2 % a year

30 Growing Gap
· This shows the growing gap between discovery and consumption as we move from surplus to deficit
· The yellow curve shows exploration drilling.
· Note that the level of activity barely affects the discovery trend. It destroys the flat earth heresy that discovery is driven by market forces

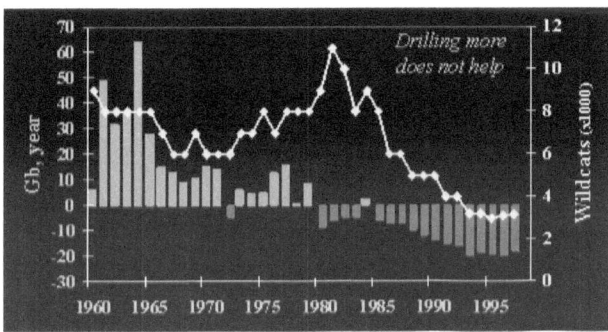

31 Spike
But this year, we did have an exceptional discovery spike.
· The underlying general trend was down to about 6 Gb
· New deepwater discovery, here treated as non-conventional, added about 4 Gb. It may well be approaching a peak too
· And there were two exceptional large finds in hitherto closed areas in the Caspian and Iran adding about 12 Gb
But even this exceptional year did not quite balance consumption

32 Depletion Examples
I would now like to quickly demonstrate a few examples of depletion

· Remember that the peak of discovery has to be followed by the peak of production
· Remember too that peak production generally comes close to the midpoint of depletion when half the total has been used.

33 US-48
Let us start with the US-48, the most mature oil country of all.
· It had plenty of money, every incentive with the oil rights in private hands and soaring imports
· It had a large prospective territory
· We can be sure that if more could have been found, it would have been found.
· So what did Nature deliver?

34 US-48 Graph
Discovery, shown in green, peaked in 1930 at the edge of the chart. Production peaked 40 years later

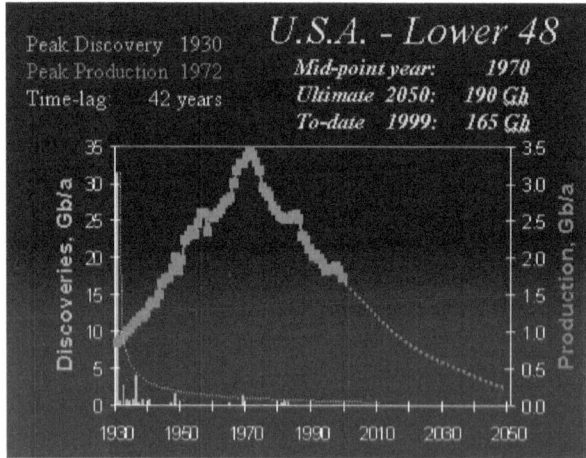

35 N.Sea graph

It is the same pattern in the North Sea, but advances in technology reduced the time lag to 27 years. We are getting better at depleting our resources.

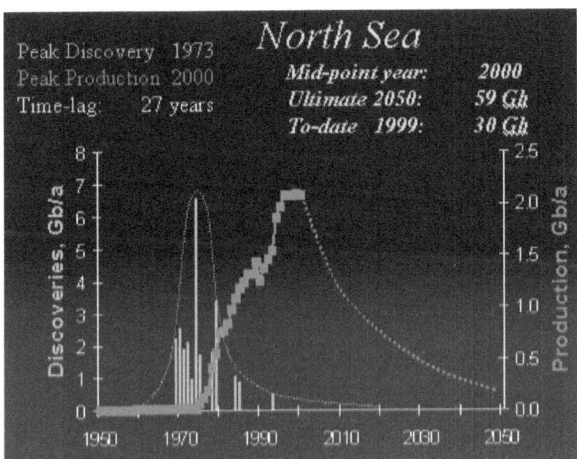

36 World graph

This is the world as a whole.

· The green bars show discovery, highlighting a few exceptional spikes in the Middle East.

· The oil shocks of the 1970s cut demand so that the actual peak came later and lower than would otherwise have been the case

· It means that the decline is less steep than it would otherwise have been

· It reminds us that if we produce less today, there is more left for tomorrow.

· It is a lesson we need to relearn as a matter of urgency.

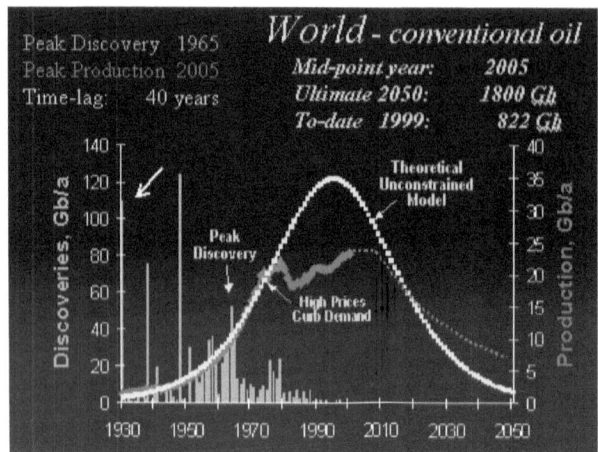

37 Distribution

This shows the distribution of oil
Note how North America has consumed most of its oil
Note how the Middle East has most of what is left

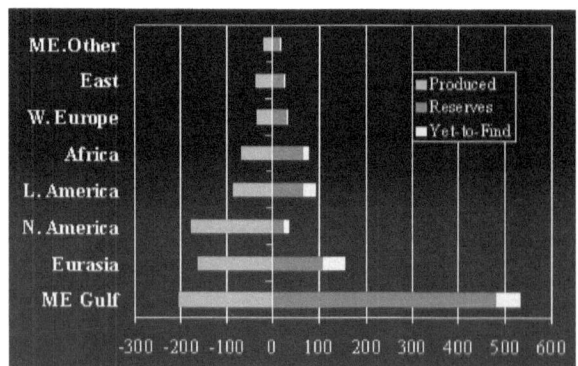

38 Swing Share

That introduces the idea of swing share
· The Five Middle East countries have been forced into a certain swing role around peak. For a certain limited period, they can - at least in

resource terms - make up the difference between world demand and what the rest of the world can produce.
· The yellow line shows their share of world production
· The green bars show price
· Share was 38% in 1973 at the time of the first oil shock
· It had fallen to 18% by 1985 because new provinces in the North Sea, Alaska and elsewhere started to deliver flush production from giant fields which are usually found first
· I stress that these new provinces had been found before the shock and were not a consequence of it as is so often claimed by flat-earth economists
· Share is now at about 30% and set to rise. This time there are no new major provinces waiting to deliver, or even in sight, save perhaps the Caspian

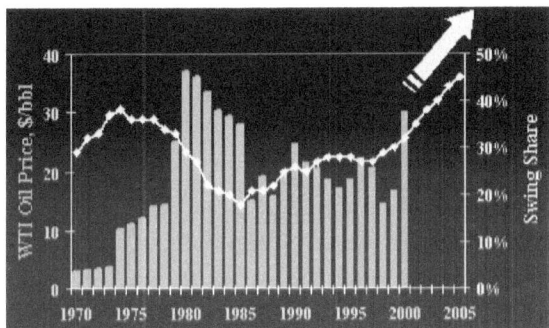

39 ME Gulf Graph
· This shows the depletion of the Middle East.
· Actual production has been far below what was possible
· Note how rapidly production will have to rise to meet demand even with that being curbed by rising price. It is optimistic to believe that such an increase can be achieved in time.

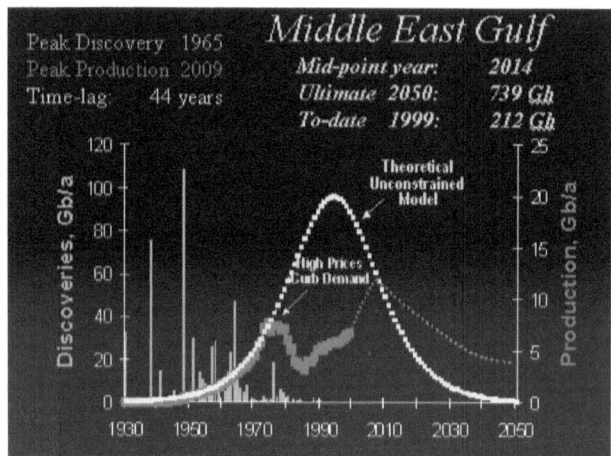

40 Expropriation

I might digress briefly to explain the impact of expropriation.
· It started with BP in Iran in 1951 but had spread to the other main producers by the 1970s.
· The major companies lost their main sources of supply.
· Had they remained in control, they would have produced the cheap and easy oil before turning to the expensive and difficult. It would have given a gradual transition as depletion began to grip
· But when they lost their main supplies, they moved to the expensive and difficult areas and they worked flat out.
· The main OPEC governments were left with the cheap and easy stuff.
· It is contrary to normal economic practice and one of the causes of the present crisis

41 Inheritance

This I think is a very compelling graph.
· The red line is discovery smoothed with a 10 year moving average
· It shows a clear downward trend, easy to extrapolate, as shown in orange

· The green line is production, extrapolated at a 2% growth to match the past trend.
· Our inheritance is the area between the red and green lines.
· We have to eat into our inheritance of past discovery because future discovery is insufficient
· There just is not enough to sustain growth, or even hold current production for long
· The blue line shows the inevitable decline

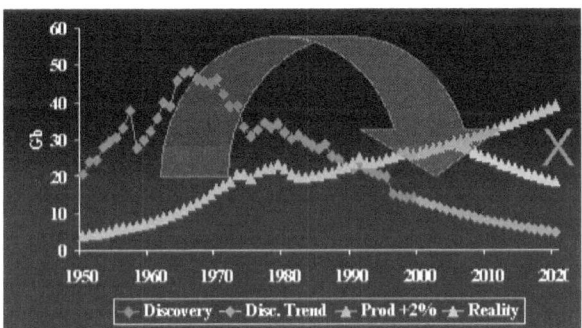

42 World depletion

This shows a production profile imposed by these known and easily understood resource constraints.
It is not prophecy. It is reality

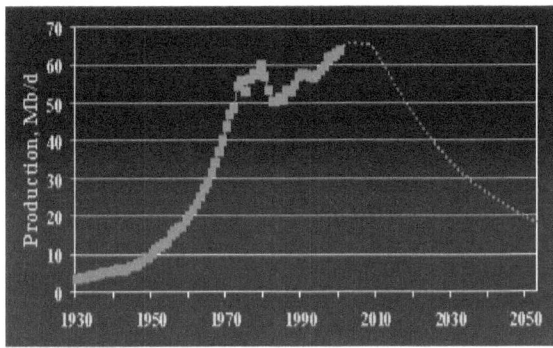

43 Two-phased Crisis
We face therefore a two-phased crisis, the first of which has already arrived, as predicted
· A price shock comes when Middle East share reaches a critical threshold, and even it cannot raise production fast enough to meet demand. Non-Middle East production falls. That is happening now.
· The second phase comes around 2010 with the onset of chronic long-term shortage, as the Middle East can no longer meet even current demand, never mind growth. By then, it will be asked to supply 50% of the world's oil, which will be beyond is ability

44 Peak dates
In short
· Conventional oil peaks around 2005
· All hydrocarbons around 2010
· Gas around 2020
· Gas liquids peak a little after gas, as extraction rates increase
· The decline after peak is about 3% a year

45 All hydrocarbons Graph
This illustrates the depletion of all hydrocarbons

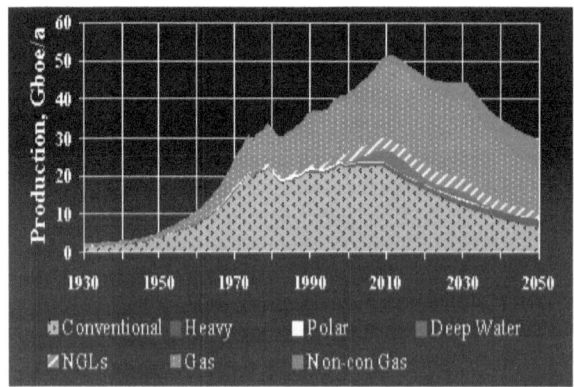

46 Denial & Obfuscation
I would now like to ask why this important subject is not better understood

47 Flat Earth
People once believed the earth was flat. Scientific observations to the contrary were treated as heresy. Look at the threatened, suspicious and hostile expressions on the faces of these mediaeval monks. They were the Establishment of the day. The same expressions are now to be found in many of the world's governments.

48 Political Reactions
We have several political reactions, which we might almost call conspiracies
· The United States seeks to exaggerate the world's oil to reduce OPEC's confidence. It pretends that it does not depend on Middle East oil. It puts out very flawed studies by the US Geological Survey and the

Department of Energy. l
· OPEC, for its part, exaggerates its resource base to inhibit non-OPEC investments and moves to energy savings or renewables. It fears a repetition of the price collapse that followed the last shocks, not realising that it is a different world.
· Companies conceal depletion because it sits badly on the investment community

49 USGS
· The USGS has failed to live up to its scientific reputation
· It has assessed the Undiscovered Potential of each basin with a range of subjective probabilities. It has a Low Case for the most sure and a High Case for the least sure. The High Case itself has little meaning. You might as well say that there is a 5% chance that I am a frog.
· The Low Case is fairly good, consistent with the discovery trend, but The Mean value, which is the one they publicise is meaningless because it is influenced by the High Case. This has been confirmed by experience in the real world because the Mean estimate is already 100 Gb short, five years into the study period
· The notion of "reserve growth" is also flawed. The USGS depicts it as a technological dynamic when it is simply an artefact of reporting practice, not to be extrapolated into the future.
· It claims that Greenland is the most prospective area, which it deems part of North America
· Statoil has now drilled a dry hole on the prime prospect

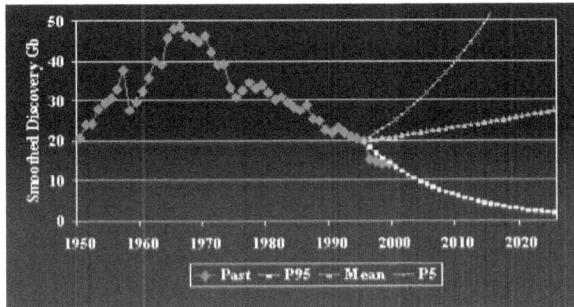

50 IEA

The International Energy Agency was established by the OECD countries in the aftermath of the shocks of the 1970s. In 1998, it succeeded in delivering a coded message.

· It showed how a "business as usual scenario" could not be fulfilled without inventing a so-called balancing item of Unidentified Unconventional, which miraculously rises from zero in 2010 to 19 Mb/d in 2020, when the identified makes a ceiling of only 2.4 by 2010. Since the identified deposits are huge, no one needs to find more. The so-called unidentified unconventional is accordingly a euphemism for rank shortage.

· Can anybody really imagine that oil price will still be $25/b when the Middle East supplies 62% of the world's needs

As a political institution it could only send a coded message and was pleased when journalists decrypted it.

51 Agip

Most companies have to sing to the stockmarket, but the Italian national company is less concerned by stockmarket imagery. Its Chairman was able to tell the truth:

· "New reserves are failing to keep up with growing output"

· "My forecast is that between 2000 and 2005 the world will be reaching peak..."

52. BP Prize
British Petroleum certainly wins the prize for the most oblique reference to depletion when it changes its logo to a sunflower and says that BP stands for Beyond Petroleum
But its executives sit on the board of Goldman Sachs, the bankers. They should accordingly know what BP actually thinks behind the lace curtains of corporate make-believe. What do the bankers say?

53 Goldman Sachs
"The rig count over the last 12 years has reached bottom. This is not because of low oil price. The oil companies are not going to keep rigs employed to drill dry holes. They know it but are unable and unwilling to admit it. The great merger mania is nothing more than a scaling down of a dying industry in recognition of the fact that 90% of global conventional oil has already been found." - Goldmann Sachs, August 1999

54 Shell
Shell says it in other words
"There was a time when oil and gas reserves seemed endless..." - November 1999 Advertisement

55 Merger Mania
Actions speak louder than words.
· The major companies and many others in the industry are merging and shedding staff
· They are also buying their own stock
· These are moves to downsize because there are no major investment opportunities left
· Their past is worth more than their future - and they know it.

56 What is all adds up to
I will try now to conclude with some general comments, starting with a oil price

57 Oil price Plot
· Oil outside the Middle East peaked in 1997 as easily foreseen.
· It should have heralded a gradual rise in price from growing Middle East control, shown in green. But instead there was an anomalous fall.
· It is a volatile unstable market that has failed to manage this critical resource.

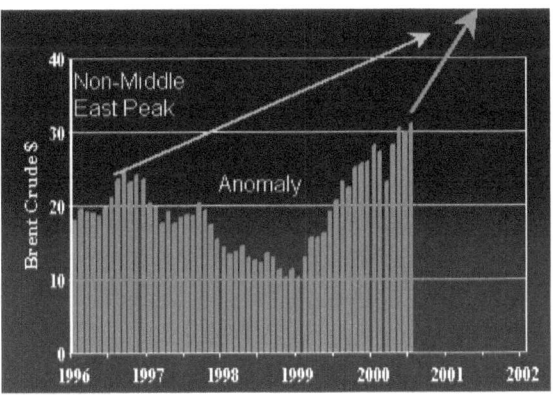

58 Oil Price Collapse
· Price collapsed in 1998 because of the interaction of warm weather, an Asian recession, the devaluation of the rouble, events in Iraq, false supply estimates by the IEA that prompted higher OPEC production and perhaps some manipulation by insiders
· Now there is a firm upward trend based on rising demand, the inability to offset natural decline in giant old fields, and falling discovery
· The market hangs on Opec's words - but Opec has lost control

59 Oil Price plot repeated
Instead of the gradual increase starting in 1997, we now face a more dramatic increase, shown in red

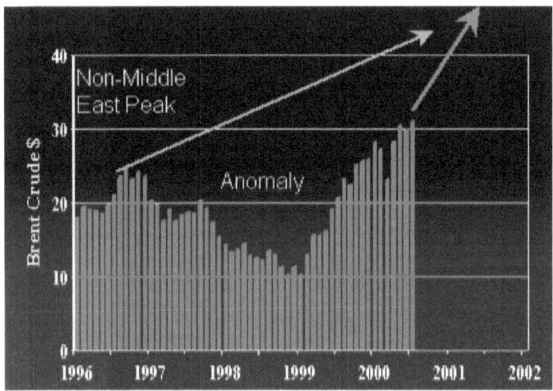

60 Spare Capacity
· Spare capacity can mean many things. A closed flowing well is the only form of spare capacity that can deliver quickly. All the other elements take investment, work and, above all, time to deliver.
· OPEC has very little operational spare capacity. It is working flat out. It has to run faster to stand still, as it desperately tries to offset the natural decline of its old fields. It will be hard pressed to meet the demands made upon it even to maintain current world production, never mind growth

61 Logical Consequences
· The market is now perceiving that OPEC has lost control. It is a devastating realisation because it means there is no supply-based ceiling on price. Accordingly, prices are set to soar. Don't forget that in to-day's money, oil price went to almost $100 in the 1970 shocks
· Demand must then fall. The poor countries of the world will bear most of the burden. But the United States will be in serious difficulties. There

is, I think, a strong danger of some ill-considered military intervention to try to secure oil. A stock market crash seems inevitable, as some investment managers are now telling us.
· The global market may collapse because of high transport costs and global recession.
· Self-sufficiency will become a priority.

Here some quick thoughts

62 Energy doesn't matter
· Economists say high oil price does not matter because energy is a smaller percent of GDP
· But you can't eat the internet

63 Geologists, engineers and economists
· Geologists find oil, engineers exploit it,
   ... beware of economists telling you how much is left

64 Political immunity
· Oil is ultimately controlled by events in the geological past
   ... which are immune to politics

65 Germany's oil
· Not everyone realises that Germany has had a long oil history. The earliest field in the database was found in 1856, before Colonel Drake drilled his famous well in Pennsylvania. About 600 wildcats have been drilled, about as many as in Norway.
· But they found only about 2.3 Gb of oil, shown as bars.
· The country has now been very thoroughly explored
· I assess its ultimate at about 2.5 Gb.
· Peak production was in 1967, ten years before the midpoint of depletion, which was in 1977.

· Production is now declining at about 3%, much less than would be the case offshore.
· Germany, like the USA, is a good example of a mature oil country whose experience is to be matched elsewhere.

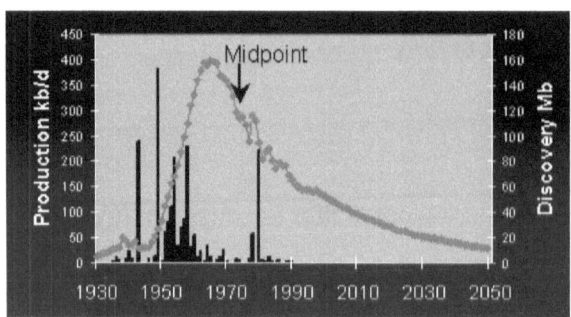

66 Germany's energy policy

Let us consider for the moment what Germany's reaction to what I have discussed should be
· Windmills and bicycles set very good examples, but there are still too many large Mercedes
· It would be a good idea to start rationing gasoline and heating fuel early to provide minimal essential needs at moderate price, perhaps by credit card. It will be a complex task to identify all the special needs of people and evolve a fair and equitable system
· There should be inverted tariffs on electricity so that the more you use the more expensive it becomes
· Germany is a large and powerful country. It should exert its influence on Brussels, which has so far failed miserably to understand the situation. As recently as October 4th it issued a report on Europe's oil supply without mentioning the resource or depletion and suggesting it was just a matter of OPEC politics. It understands nothing.
· Germany should revitalise the BGR to resume the excellent studies, which were undertaken under the previous Director. They were I

believe suppressed by the Ministry of Economics, who did not want to know the truth.
· Germany should resist Green pressure to give up nuclear power at precisely the moment it needs more energy, as oil peaks and declines.
· Germany has coal and possibilities for coalbed methane. This industry needs to be rediscovered. It may become economic again
· Germany should encourage its motor manufacturers to move to more efficient engines and hydrogen fuels, especially those made by solar means. It should provide whatever fiscal incentives are needed.
· Germany is in a position to take a lead. It should use its strength to do so.

67 Depletion Protocol
Germany should support the idea of a Depletion Protocol whereby the consumers as well as the producers would manage depletion
· It could be easily added to an existing OECD treaty that established the International Energy Agency
· It would provide that no country would produce above its present depletion rate
· No country would import any infringement
· It would bring order and cooperation
· And has been welcomed by the OPEC Secretary General

68 Political Response
An oil crisis is bad for politicians.
· Blaming OPEC or the oil companies will not wash much longer.
· It would be better to make a proper analysis of the true position and inform people.
· No one blames the government for an earthquake. So they would n't blame it for an oil crisis either if they realised it was a natural phenomenon
"If you don't deal with reality, reality will deal with you"

69 Sky does not fall in at Peak
· Let us not be too alarmist. The roof does not fall in at peak. What changes are perceptions, as people come to realise that the growth of the past becomes the decline of the future.
· It may herald the end of the US economic and cultural hegemony - which some people might think was no bad thing
· Climate concerns recede
· But let us use our current high oil supply intelligently while it lasts to ease the transition

70 More efficient vehicles
· For example, much more efficient vehicles have already been designed
· The government should encourage their use by penalising inefficient vehicles with high tax

71 Conclusions
· Peak oil is a turning point for Mankind
· 100 years of easy growth ends
· Population peaks too for not unrelated reasons
· The transition to decline is a period of great tension

- Priorities shift to self-sufficiency and sustainability
- It may end up a better world

STRENGTH

The strengths of this article are numerous: the true state of depletion as it is happening in the Middle East, in Europe and in Africa. The oil companies making huge profits from crude oil at the detriment of the local indigenes; these local people have been cheated of the real benefits of their natural resources. The oil workers are being used as slave workers, receiving very little wages while the executives, doing virtually nothing, are rewarded with billions of dollars. The various governments of these countries with crude oil are not distributing the revenues from the oil equitably amongst its people. For instance, about 30% of the youths in Saudi Arabia are unemployed, jobless and uneducated. These youths were among the people recruited by the terrorist groups on 9/11/2001 to destroy the United States. The situation is worse in Nigeria.

This article was well researched and the facts are as solid as the Rock of Gibraltar!

WEAKNESS

The writer here did not cite specific incidences or conflicts in all major oil producing countries. The article did not cite in details the roles of industrialized countries and American interests in the control and conflicts involved in producing and distribution of crude oil all over the world. The author did not discuss the current struggles for Africa crude oil and natural resources (just like the USA and USSR in the 20th century) between two great powers in the 21st century, China and the United States. And when two giant elephants fight, it is the grass that suffers! The author did not discuss the complexity of the underground maneuvering in oil trade and the criminal activities and lives lost every second, and so much more.

Nonetheless, the article is superb in its entirety. I hope you all enjoy it. I shall be writing about these issues in my dissertation.

Take good care of yourself, eat balanced diet, lots of fruits and **vegetables, and drink water daily, exercise daily, please fall in love have good sex more frequently, keep good friends who are ready to be educated and work hard in life to earn enough money to enjoy their lives, be friendly with everyone regardless of race, gender, ethnicity, greed or religion, make everyone your friend and your family, give to the poor always, help the needy always, be the first to say hello to friends and strangers, be smart and stay away from trouble always, talk less, listen more, better yourself daily, improve your life daily, forgive always, respect and protect girls and women always, laugh daily and be around happy people, do humor, take life easy, enjoy life while it lasts, go out and get the millions of dollars waiting for you, since no one is born to be poor, get education and seek information daily, be rich in morality, do those things that are excellent, and have lots, and lots of fun! Bye!**

Intentionally left blank

HOW TO BE A GREAT MANAGER AND A GREAT LEADER BOTH AT THE WORK PLACE & AT HOME (PART 10)

PART TEN (NOTE: SO MANY SERIES COMING IN THE FUTURE)

By Prince Gabriel

Hon. Member US Army, MBA, Doctorate in Management

JD Candidate

Copyright ©Prince Gabriel 2011

INTRODUCTION

If you are well educated and licensed in your field of work, or if you have a lot of years of experiences in that field, and you know how to do your job very well, equally with your peers, or better, then you would have earned the authority of your peers and your subordinates or workers below you. Regardless of whether or not you are so perfect at what you do, or that you know how to do anything so well, great leaders are constantly looking for ways to improve daily through training, education, and so on. It is called the relentless pursuit of perfection and excellence. It is like being a superman or a superwoman. Even when everything seems to be working well you and your people are constantly experimenting and exploring novel ideas and innovative ways to get better and improve. Always! **Change**

things for the better. Change things around, and ***put square pegs in square holes***. Do not change things for the sake of just changing things. Make sure the change is necessary, relevant and productive. Sometimes change takes time. Be consistent. Persevere. ***Cooperate and compromise with the conservative elements in society who may have good reasons for resisting change***. That is one of the ways you earn your authority. There are several other ways you earn your authority.

Suppose you are the manager or leader of an organization/corporation or a nation. You are also a great cook. (I encourage every leader out there to learn the art of cooking great food. Cooking encourages one to have patience, since good food takes time to cook, and the art of putting the right ingredients together, through diligence, practices, learning, and so on, makes one to be versatile. A great manager/leader should be capable of doing many things competently. That is a truism. It's extremely important for the unity of the family at home and for friends, friendship, and for getting different people together, in harmony, love, bonding, camaraderie, and so on). That is to say, you know how to cook delicious food. You can cook good food for your families at home and make them happy. Isn't that great!

So, one day you ask everyone to come for a free meal, free drinks and gifts for everyone, especially those workers or people who are naturally motivated to work hard and produce great results/profits without any push or promise of anything.

So, you serve your workers or your people with different variety of very good foods that you have cooked. The people eat your food, praise you for being a great cook, drink your wine and juice and water and get full satisfaction from this kind of generosity and hospitality. Any manager/leader out there who can cook good food that everybody can eat and get real satisfaction has done a great thing to get to the minds and souls of his/her workers and earned that elusive word "authority" and most importantly the admiration of your workers and your people.

You can get your artificial authority through various means: from the government, by law, from the Human Resources of an Organization, through promotions, and so on. However, the natural authority, the actual authority, comes from being generous and considerate, doing natural things like cooking for everyone or buying great dinner or lunch for everyone, or giving free gifts, gift certificates or company stocks, or bonus checks that can easily be converted into cash; since most people would prefer cash and money, especially during the time of economic recession. Note very carefully: be transparent, be open, let there be no hidden agenda in the course of you doing good and helping others. Maintain the highest level of honesty and integrity. That is how you earn your authority.

My dear managers and leaders out there: life is already very hard for a lot of folks out there. Do not do anything to contribute to that hardship. Rather try everything humanly possible to reverse the harsh situations for the better for everyone, within the Rule of Law or justice and/or equity. Please. Try. Try. Try. Make good things happen for everyone. Yes, you can do it!

CHAPTER ONE

Leadership is both an art and a science. In fact, leadership is much more than art and science. It is unity, peace and stability of people in society. It is the net good to your organization and/or society. Leadership is constantly discovering and evolving. Leadership is innovation. It is quality of the highest level or degree. Leadership is also quantity. It is great customer service; any good action that exceeds one's expectations. Leadership is moral excellence. It is the relentless pursuit of perfection, excellence and outstanding performances. Leadership is being humble and innocent like a little child. It is natural, just, equitable, and maintains good conscience at all times. It is a lot more as we shall see in our future writings and discourses.

Suffice to say here that if you want to be a great manager and a great leader, I would advise you to study history, mathematics, geography, political sciences, business administration, serve in the Military, study English, French, Mandarin, Hispanics, Spanish language, Russian languages, African languages, Persian, Arabic, Physics, Chemistry, Hausa, Ibo, Yoruba, Edo, Geology, the sciences, arts and humanities, and forget about being a great leader or a great manager. Got it?

God bless you all!

Take good care of yourself, eat balanced diet, lots of fruits and vegetables, and drink clean water daily, exercise daily, please fall in love have good sex more frequently, keep good friends who are ready to be educated and work hard in life to earn enough money to enjoy their lives, be friendly with everyone regardless of race, gender, ethnicity, greed or religion, make everyone your friend and your family, give to the poor always, get at least 8 hours of sleep daily, help the needy always, be the first to say hello to friends and strangers, be smart and stay away from trouble always, talk less, listen more, better yourself daily, improve your life daily, forgive always, respect and protect girls and women always, laugh daily and be around happy people, do humor, take life easy, enjoy life while it lasts, go out and get the millions of dollars waiting for you, since no one is born to be poor, get education and seek information daily, be rich in morality, do those things that are excellent, and have lots, and lots of fun! Bye!

Intentionally left blank

This is Gabriel Atsepoyi, an American Soldier. He studied Law (LL.B), BA History, MBA and a Doctorate Degrees in Management. (Univ of Colorado, Cambridge, etc). **If you have special talent and you want sponsorship to the USA or any country, please get in touch with me pronto**. You can also consult me for Leadership ideas, and ways to improve any government or corporation. **I am ready and able to help the USA Government or Nigeria Government anytime. Please call me! 720 934 1983 USA.**

CONTACT ME ANYTIME: Gabriel.atsepoyi@yahoo.com Or gatsepoyi@gmail.com

Telephone number in the United States: 720 934 1983

Or write to me regarding any other business you wish to do with me, like Wealth Management, Partnerships, or any issue, etc. Send your letters to:

Gabriel B. Atsepoyi

Doctorate program

5775 DTC BLVD, SUITE 100

GREENWOOD VILLAGE, COLORADO 80111 USA

FAX 303 694 6673

THE BOOK OF TOTAL HAPPINESS
by Gabriel B. Atsepoyi (Akpieyi)

Education is the key to learning any subject better, so why should it be any different when it comes to being happy? This is the premise for Gabriel Atsepoyi's *The Book of Total Happiness*, in which the author gives new meaning to the search for happiness and contentment in one's life.

It has been said that psychological maturity is achieved when one gains a secure understanding of the meaning of life and one's place in it. This fascinating volume explores this matter in full detail concerning happiness, marriage, health and physical well-being. Regardless of religious or philosophical persuasion, readers will become engrossed in this presentation, which to its credit does not intend to talk down to readers, but instead provides working guidelines in a straightforward and easily understood fashion.

Given the high rate of divorce these days, Mr. Atsepoyi believes that without some form of education concerning marriage, the do's and don't's, the expectations and the compromises, people are destined to continue to allow this shocking statistic to grow. This book's goal, therefore, is to begin that education, to provide understandable paths toward that elusive spiritual habitat, being happy. It's not as easy as it seems, says the author, and most people have to work at it. Yet, it is not totally out of reach, if one can look at life with honest appraisal and work to change those things that hinder one's happiness.

One of the more intriguing aspects of this book is the point that not everyone achieves the same level of happiness, nor has the same avenues available to them in their search for personal happiness. That is fine, says the author, because no two people are exactly the same. Each must find that place that is comfortable for him or her, then work to maintain those good feelings through effort and commitment.

Mr. Atsepoyi's prose is fluid and expressive, and his observations are shrewdly punctuated by a basic wisdom that will appeal to all. But what makes this book be singled out from the many is the significant contribution it makes toward re-educating people of the how and why of being happy. This serves a most practical purpose, first in helping the reader to find paths and guidelines for being happy, the author is also boldly illustrating the power of individual expression, positive thinking, and having a goal to work toward.

Highly recommended for its insight and analyses, *The Book of Total Happiness*, by Gabriel Atsepoyi, is must reading. The author's ideas are lucid and innovative, portraying much wisdom and common sense, and combining all these attributes into one volume enables each reader to further his or her education on perhaps the most important subject matter existing today, the art of being happy.

Section Two of the book focuses on: A-Z about HIV/AIDS and the latest facts on AIDS, protection for kids and family, women's rights (the need to respect and protect women), smoking and its hazards, environmental protection/prevention, how and the need for better education for children, etc. etc.

THE BOOK OF TOTAL HAPPINESS
ABOUT THE AUTHOR

Gabriel Atsepoyi (Akpieyi), twenty-six years old, was born in Africa and presently resides in Colorado.

An avid reader, Mr. Atsepoyi makes it known that the only way he is happy is when he is helping others. His love of God serves his existence well, as he expands upon his belief that one's knowledge is one's power in leading a happy and successful life.

A member of the Optimist Club of Arvada, the author has had many articles published previously on a variety of topics, yet his overriding concerns are for the rate of divorce and its effects toward broken homes, unhappy families, neglected children, uneducated and uncultured children, and crime. He has propounded many solutions in these areas in his latest work, and his hope is that readers will reflect upon those suggestions.

THE BOOK OF TOTAL HAPPINESS
by Gabriel B. Atsepoyi (Akpieyi)

Education is the key to learning any subject better, so why should it be any different when it comes to being happy? This is the premise for Gabriel Atsepoyi's *The Book of Total Happiness*, in which the author gives new meaning to the search for happiness and contentment in one's life.

It has been said that psychological maturity is achieved when one gains a secure understanding of the meaning of life and one's place in it. This fascinating volume explores this matter in full detail concerning happiness, marriage, health and physical well-being. Regardless of religious or philosophical persuasion, readers will become engrossed in this presentation, which to its credit does not intend to talk down to readers, but instead provides working guidelines in a straightforward and easily understood fashion.

Given the high rate of divorce these days, Mr. Atsepoyi believes that without some form of education concerning marriage, the do's and don't's, the expectations and the compromises, people are destined to continue to allow this shocking statistic to grow. His book's goal, therefore, is to begin that education, to provide understandable paths toward that elusive spiritual habitat, being happy. It's not as easy as it seems, says the author, and most people have to work at it, but it is not totally out of reach, if one can look at life with honest appraisal and work to change those things that hinder one's happiness.

One of the more intriguing aspects of the book is the point that not everyone achieves the same level of happiness, nor has the same avenues available to them in their search for personal happiness. That is fine, says the author, because no two people are exactly the same. Each must fine that place that is comfortable for him or her, then work to maintain those good feelings through effort and commitment.

Mr. Atsepoyi's prose is fluid and expressive, and his observations are shrewdly punctuated by a basic wisdom that will appeal to all. But what makes this book be singled out from the many is the significant contribution it makes toward re-educating people of the how and why of being happy. This serves a most practical purpose, first in helping the reader to find paths and guidelines for being happy, the author is also boldly illustrating the power of individual expression, positive thinking, and having a goal to work toward.

Highly recommended for its insight and analyses, *The Book of Total Happiness*, by Gabriel Atsepoyi, is must reading. The author's ideas are lucid and innovative, portraying much wisdom and common sense, and combining all these attributes into one volume enables each reader to further his or her education on perhaps the most important subject matter existing today, the art of being happy.

Section Two of the book focuses on: A-Z about HIV/AIDS and the latest facts on AIDS, protection for kids and family, women's rights (the need to respect and protect women), smoking and its hazards, environmental protection/prevention, how and the need for better education for children, etc., etc.

THE BOOK OF TOTAL HAPPINESS

ABOUT THE AUTHOR

Gabriel Atsepoyi (Akpieyi), twenty-six years old, was born in Africa and presently resides in Colorado.

An avid reader, Mr. Atsepoyi makes it known that the only way he is happy is when he is helping others. His love of God serves his existence well as he expands upon his belief that one's knowledge is one's power in leading a happy and successful life.

A member of the Optimist Club of Arvada, the author has had many articles published previously on a variety of topics, yet his overriding concerns are for the rate of divorce and its effects toward broken homes, unhappy families, neglected children, uneducated and uncultured children, and crime. He has propounded many solutions in these areas in his latest work, and his hope is that readers will reflect upon those suggestions.

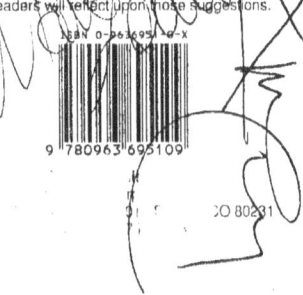

Can you give hopes to people? Can you help make those hopes real? <u>Can you help to actualize hopes for humans? Can you?</u>

Take good care of yourself, eat balanced diet, lots of fruits and vegetables, and drink water daily, exercise daily, please fall in love have good sex more frequently, keep good friends who are ready to be educated and work hard in life to enjoy their lives, be friendly with everyone regardless of race, gender, ethnicity, greed or religion, make everyone your friend and your family, give to the poor always, help the needy always, be the first to say hello to friends and strangers, be smart and stay away from trouble always, talk less, listen more, better yourself daily, improve your life daily, forgive always, respect and protect girls and women always, laugh daily and be around happy people, do humor, take life easy, enjoy life while it lasts, go out and get the millions of dollars waiting for you, since no one is born to be poor, get education and seek information daily, be rich in morality, do those things that are excellent, and have lots, and lots of fun! Bye!

Can you give hopes to people? Can you help make those hopes real? <u>Can you help to actualize hopes for humans? Can you?</u>

August 20, 1993

Mr. Gabriel B. Atsepoyi
8826 E. Florida Ave. #101
Denver, CO 80231

Dear Mr. Atsepoyi,

It was such a delight to receive your book Total Happiness. I am grateful. Your kindness and thoughtfulness are appreciated.

Again, thank you for thinking of me.

Best wishes,

Oprah Winfrey

OW:sb

Prince Gabriel, Africa

Intentionally left blank

PEACE: specific things to do to have peace

If world peace you crave, world peace you shall get. If national peace you want, national peace you shall get. If you want peace within yourself or peace with others, (you must have inner peace before you can have peace with others, a must!), the peace you so crave is within reach.

I have traveled widely because I am an American Soldier. I have seen a lot over the years. I see two giant elephants struggling everyday for domination of the scarce natural resources, and for power. And when two giant elephants struggle or fight, it is the grass (that is, the ordinary poor people, like in Africa) that suffers! Who are these two giant elephants? They are China and the United States.

I hope you would take the time to travel around the world too and meet with people, make friends, love, respect other people's culture and norms and cherish other people's ways of doing things, try other people's food, experience other people's cultures and <u>live in harmony with one another</u>.

I spent the first twenty years of my life traveling all over Africa, and the other twenty years of my life in the United States, Europe and Asia. This is my observation for the past forty years or so. I learn over the years you cannot force people to do anything against their wish. It is through reason, begging, cajoling, fairness, justice, and sometimes appealing to emotion, by crying, using children and women to plead and beg others to listen to reason, that you can get people to see reason and do what is right, morally and legally. Not war. (Please see all my books below).

I love the people in Europe. Europe is a product of history, unlike the United States that is a product of philosophy, (the idea of freedom). The people in Europe are beautiful people. The people in Europe are good people. The people of Europe are very smart people. The continent of Europe has had so many wars in the past. I thought they would be tired of wars by now. I was wrong. Now, there is a new war in Libya, championed first by the United States, and now Europe or NATO just took over the Libya war. Both the United States and its NATO Alliance or countries in Europe, or European Union (EU) have good intentions: both the USA and EU are doing the best they can to save humankind and help the poor countries. Why Libya, though? The same thing happening in Libya is happening in Syria, Jordan, Saudi Arabia, almost everywhere in the Arab world, and perhaps, very soon, the poor people in the world will start a revolution in all countries in the world. <u>Is war the answer to the plight of the poor</u> and the problems all over the world? There are earthquakes and tsunamis in Japan, Haiti, Katrina (in the USA), South America, Africa, China, Australia, in fact, catastrophe in every corner of the globe. Is war the answer? Or is war compounding everything? Well, time will tell.

On the other hand of the equation is China. While Europe and United States are squandering their wealth and natural resources in wars and conflicts, China is busy accumulating wealth and improving every aspect of the Chinese economy, amidst human rights abuse with impunity. China and India have more than two billion people. Land is scarce in both countries. Natural resource is very scarce in both China and India, and the demand for natural resource, and/or food far exceeds the supply. What is going to happen in India and China? Well, time will tell. Suffice to say right now there are sweat shops in China and India, and in all poor countries, with the poor people working all day and night for pennies, amidst diseases, hunger, starvation, wars, conflicts and natural disasters. I can tell you there is global revolution looming. Trust me.

China is a great country. I love Chinese people, really! I love everything that is China. I love Chinese cultures, food, traditions and norms. Chinese people are beautiful people. Chinese people are great people, culturally.

I love Africa. I love African people. The Africans are good people. The Africans are beautiful people.

They are victims of some known and unknown circumstances. I wish Africans will get their house together, sooner than later, give everyone free quality and quantity education and improve every aspect of the African lives. Well, time will tell.

I love the United States of America. I love the beautiful American people. The United States of America is one of the best countries in the world! United States is an excellent country because it champions human rights abuses, polices the world to do good things, feeds the poor, most important, the United States has the Bill of Rights in its

Constitution to do what is right legally and morally, however, racism is perhaps legal in the United States. Nonetheless, the United States is a place to be anytime. The United States has the best security for your life, <u>sometimes</u>. The USA is, perhaps, the best country to be, if you are coming to hustle for a living. That is a truism.

It is very easy to have world peace: we all just need to come back to nature (<u>with a clean hand</u>, honesty, sincerity, <u>ready to do justice</u>, fairness and equality), from whose bosom we all emanated.

If you see a naked man/woman running around naked, with no clothes on, first, you put on your clothes before you run around to help that mad person. If you run around naked, like the mad man/woman, you become a mad person yourself. See that!

However, a mad person running around naked has gone back to nature. Why can't we all get naked publicly and shout and scream, without making any sense like a mad person. In other words please <u>reverse</u> (in a very funny, unique way, I will show you how later) every solution or idea you have used for years that have failed you in getting peace and see what I mean here.

We have lived on this earth for over ten thousand years according to scientific data available everywhere now that it is common knowledge (at least in the Western World). We have tried to make sense of everything but to no avail. The world has never been able to see peace.

In this book, I am here to propose novel, innovative, and unique ideas for personal peace and/or national peace and/or world peace.

Chapter One

The Clinton Example

Bill and Hilary Clinton just celebrated the marriage of their only daughter, Chelsea (a Christian), to a long-time boy friend, Marc Mezvinsky, Jewish, because Chelsea and Marc are deeply in love with each other! Isn't this the way nature has intended things to be? I think that is in accordance with natural law, equity and good conscience. That is to say: move out of your comfort zone and meet different people on the other side of the isle. If you are rich or wealthy, please marry a poor person and vice versa. It is time too for a woman to become President of the United States and Secretary-General of the United Nations, etc. Please let us *reverse* all the ways we have been handling world problems for us to have everlasting, true and real, peace. Please! The feelings of love, unity, peace, progress, togetherness, and camaraderie can sometimes be exhilarating, just to say the least.

Perhaps leaders of the world like Benjamin Netanyahu (and other leaders in Israel too) should <u>please</u> allow his children to get out of his culture and religion freely and mingle with the Moslems and vice versa; perhaps, something strong and tight might happen. Perhaps a marriage (like Chelsea and Marc) or a deeper bond might seal the disagreements between the Israelis and the Palestinians. It is time to reverse our approach and ideas hitherto, and try the opposites.

In the case of North Korea, Iran, the United States and the rest of the world, perhaps the President of the United States should invite the current Presidents of North Korea and Iran (separately) to the White House for a dinner! Talk heart to heart with people on equal and/or just terms, naturally. Find common ground naturally, meet more frequently, exchange gifts, compromise, while seating face to face, touch each other with permission, become friends forever, seal your friendship with something unbreakable naturally, something as strong and valuable like diamonds, marriage, etc. Come back to nature people! You have all strayed away from nature for too long.

Please come back to nature my dear brothers and sisters. I speak to you as nobody, but, please listen to me World Leaders! Please come back to nature and have everlasting Peace. Please!!!

You see, human beings are necessarily good. Whenever you isolate people or tag people or disrespect people (in any form or shape) or oppress people, people are going to act up. I hope somebody is listening. Reverse your tactics please.

Chapter Two

War is a Waste. Use the money to build life…

The billions and trillions of dollars spent in the Gulf Wars, in Afghanistan, Libya and the endless wars in the world currently could transform the entire civilization of the world, if the same amount of money is spent diligently in building schools, roads, colleges, training teachers, and given freely to all the poor people in the world to better themselves.

Please let us reverse the current approaches to solving problems as we journey progressively into the future.

The following suggestions should be taken seriously. Please.

1. Instead of Congress declaring war in the United States, the citizens of the United States should be asked first in a referendum to declare war; a 2/3 vote in favor should be required to go to any war in the future. With that 2/3 in favor then Congress can declare war. Natural law requires every American to be consulted

formally before any future war is declared because America is wasting its talents and natural resources through countless, unnecessary wars. Although, I am nobody right now, please listen to me because I served with HONORS in the United States Army. <u>Thank you for listening</u>.

2. We all need to get back to nature and become selfless and happy again. We all need natural love and affection, naturally. Happy and selfless people always do peace. Happy and generous people will feed the hungry and needy people

of the world. Unless we feed the poor and needy people of the world and teach everyone how to fish independently (that is help everyone, help every poor person to become educated, free from diseases, and be financially and economically balanced in life, and then become self-reliant), unless that, there can be no *real* peace.

Chapter Three

People Swap, in a Super-Continent or within a nation

Just imagine for a moment that once a year all the poor people in poor countries are swapped with all the rich peoples in rich countries(or even within the United States, for instance), for sort of a role play! Wouldn't that be fun!

Or, let's say all the members of the Taliban and *al Qaeda* (since Osama Bin Laden is dead) are allowed free tickets in a first class seat to fly to the United States and Europe (to convince them that people in these countries are good people like them); and while there these people are given free tickets to Disney World and/or Disney Land, treated to a life of affluence and enjoyment, free cruise around the world, the finest of wine and beautiful girls in bikinis (if that is ok with them, without disrespecting them) are provided free of charge; in short all the best things in life are provided free of charge for these people! And while these Taliban people are away on free holidays in the Western World their countries are turned into heaven on earth, roads well constructed and paved like in London or in the

United States, schools are built, every part of the city and town is well planned and constructed, free homes are built for all the people (not war!), and at least ten billion dollars is provided in cash money free of charge for all the people to start a new life and better their lives! Could somebody please try my panacea here and see wonders working and everlasting peace once and forever, for the first time ever. Please! And please don't ask me where the money for this endless enjoyment for the people on the other side of the isle is coming from. We only need less that 1% of the trillions we are currently wasting in endless wars around the globe to treat these people to great life and permanent enjoyment and change their thinking and ideology for good. Well, if we are serious about *World Peace* this is a panacea that is natural, practical and realistic. Please hear me out my dear brothers and sisters out there. Please listen to me World Leaders! The world cannot go on like this peacefully! Everything is so unnatural. Please stop these wars and conflicts! We need to adopt my idea of "people swap" in a super-continental system or within any nation, where people end up in role play: the rich should endure some poverty for few weeks/months, while all the poor people should move into the homes of the rich. That's natural! That is one of the best ways to everlasting peace! During the role play the poor and the rich should be allowed to take whatever she/he likes and keep all the things she/he is able to carry away. Wouldn't that be wonderful, people! Isn't that the way nature has decreed this life to be?! Please tell me any better ways to resolve inequality, injustice, oppression and hence lack of peace in this world! Please tell me, I am listening!

One of the **best innovative ideas for peace** is presented below in the building of a viable nation or organization. I am absolutely convinced any nation or organization that wants to survive the current revolution in the Arab World, coming soon to your country, will adopt and modify almost all my ideas below. I hope somebody is listening! God bless you!

Epilogue

The **building of a nation or an organization:** using green initiatives and other sustainable economic/business practices, first-class education, that is, education with real life application, and taking care of all the people in that nation or organization financially and otherwise, etc.

Below is **Nigeria being used as an example only**:

I have a **vision** to rescue Nigeria's economy, by investing heavily in science and technology with our oil money, establishing new universities, the equivalent of Harvard, Yale, MIT and Oxford or better, in the rural areas of Nigeria, to pull people from the congested cities to a more siren, natural environment in the rural areas, to establish a state-of-the-art science laboratory attached to these new universities in the rural areas, establish farm and manufacturing plant to be attached to every university in Nigeria, because everything taught in the new Nigerian schools, colleges and universities must have real life applications to the students, and most important, to establish a Federal and

State agencies for the protection of the environment, from pollution and damage to our ecology and our environment, with strict enforcement and punitive measures for violators, because my leadership is going to protect Nigeria's fresh water (both underground water, surface water, etc), and establish beautiful National Parks all over the new Nigeria and under my leadership in the new Nigeria, the government is going to <u>invest heavily in fresh water (as the next equivalent of crude oil) and export it to countries all over the world</u>, as a major source of revenue. Also, by providing free education, the equivalent of the education at Harvard and Oxford universities, or better, for all Nigerians to get a professional degree or skill and to get free monthly allowance of $100-$500, plus free feeding and accommodations for all the students while in the university, to share the oil wealth with all Nigerians by giving out grants of $2,500 to $6,500 to all Nigerians who cannot attend the university, to start a business and become self-reliant, to provide for all Nigerians with the oil wealth by giving monthly allowance of $100-$500 to all disabled people and all old people of 65 years and above with no source of income, to invest heavily in science, technology, agriculture, infrastructures, eliminate crime almost to zero level, by making everyone in the new Nigeria well educated and well taken care of financially, and placing so much emphasis on integrity, morality and ethics (that is, doing only what is excellent, doing what is right, legally and morally) and thereafter bring American big corporations, Chinese corporations and European corporations to outsource into Nigeria's economy with friendly rules and without any tax if they commit to help our economy, to develop the Nigerian economy to be on the same level with the United States in about four years with the help of Nigerians and with the help of some of the best engineers and scientists in the United States Army (where I am a member) and/or in the United States society, and thereby making Nigeria and the

United States of America have unbreakable bonds, economically, politically, socially and otherwise.

<u>I am the only one best qualified and best suited to **change** everything for the better</u> and fix every problem in Nigeria and modernize the country to be like the United States or better.

Why do I care? I care because I love Nigeria, and I love Nigerians deeply. I love Nigeria with every fiber in my being. I weep so much daily at the cutting edge technology everywhere, (even in developing countries like South Africa, Brazil, China and India) and the rate at which the world is moving ahead so fast, technologically, yet my beloved Nigeria is so backward in everything. I could remain in the United States and enjoy my retirement from the US Army and travel all over the world with my family, but I would not do that, I just could not do that. There are too many square pegs in round holes in Nigeria. My conscience would not allow me to watch my dear brothers and sisters in my beloved Nigeria waste away, amidst the scientific and technological revolutions in the United States, Europe, Asia, China, India, and even in South Africa! As President, all I want for a salary is $1 annually! Yes, one dollar! I just need to solve Nigerian problems and turn everything around for the better within few months, that's all! I will also challenge all <u>lawmakers in the new Nigeria and all government employees to join me in the austerity measures,</u> to take a drastic pay-cut, curtail government wastes and unnecessary spending, and <u>together</u> we can save a lot of money to take concrete steps and actions to make all these promises to happen and turn Nigeria around overnight, economically, politically and socially. Yes, <u>together</u>, we can do it!

With the help of Nigerians and with the help of the United States Government, Nigeria will have its own Silicon Valley and become the best tourist center in Africa, because under my leadership every Nigerian will be very happy, with opportunities created for all Nigerians to make a lot of money, have self respect and confidence in themselves, and crime will be almost zero.

Below are my qualifications and experience for the past forty years or so. I am the author of more than forty books (available in bookstores worldwide), including, (1) *How to be a great manager/leader, Vols. 1-10, (2) Specific things to do to have World Peace, Vol. 1, (3) Chevron & Ethics, Vols. 1-*

4, (4) An American Soldier Protesting Bad Treatment to Women, Children & The Poor," (a classic), (5) Dating: Dos & Don'ts during Courtship, (6) Family & Security from Thief, (7) Fun Programs to Make Youths Productive, (8) The Secrets of Happy Family, and so many other great books.

I was born at Ugborodo Village in 1967, educated at Ugborodo Primary School (1970-1976), Ogidigben Grammar School

(1976-1979), Essi College, Warri (1979-1982), Boys' Presbyterian Secondary School, Legon, Accra, Ghana, in the Advanced Level, or A/L, 1983-1985, University of Lagos, Law, (1986-1990), Denver Technical College, Masters in Project Management, (1990-1999), United States Army, (2000-2008, active and reserve duties for six years, 2000-2006), University of Colorado, 2000-2007, BA History, MBA (2008-2009),

Colorado, *Juris Doctor*, or JD Boston, (2010-2011, pending), Doctorate in Management, Colorado, (2009-2011 pending), etc.

The Reality in Nigeria today

Nigeria's ship is sinking fast. The fundamentals of the Nigerian economy (education, infrastructures, Agriculture, Science and technology, etc) are completely broken, outdated and in a state of decadent paralysis. The economy is in dire need of a strong *turbocharger* to jerk the economy up, and/or <u>a well educated, strong leader with local and global experiences and connections like me</u>, or a sort of <u>magic touch</u> and <u>human touch</u>, possessed only by me, <u>an American Soldier, with military discipline, special knowledge and experiences</u>, acquired both in Nigeria, in Africa, in the United States, Europe and

Asia, which no leader or prospective leader in Nigeria has.

SPECIFIC THINGS I WILL DO FOR NIGERIANS

1. First and foremost: Nigeria currently is divided. Nigeria should be united wholeheartedly, north, south, east and

west. I will do it well by allowing for a Co-President. <u>If the Executive President is from the south, I will propose having a</u> **<u>co-president from the north (who must be a woman)</u>**, if the President is a man, and *vice versa*, with ceremonial title. There will be <u>enough vice-presidents to represent all tribes or class of people in Nigeria,</u> and ought to be <u>male and female vice-presidents</u>! The Nigerian

Constitution ought to be amended to include every tribe or to **include every class of people** at or near the top, in power sharing, like in Google, Microsoft or the Obama White House, thus making every Nigerian have a stake in the system, to contribute positively and progressively.

2. Education is going to be free on all levels and students will be fed free, three

times daily, plus free accommodations. Those who agree to be educated professionally will be paid free monthly allowance of $100-$500 until graduation before being helped with a lump sum by the new government to settle down. All other Nigerians who do not wish to be educated, or for whatever reason cannot attend the university, the new government is still going to share the oil wealth with all Nigerians not in the university, by giving the old or senior citizens and disabled people monthly allowance of $100-$500, while other Nigerians wanting to go into small business ventures will get a one-time grant of $2,500 to $6,500. The Money for this project is coming from natural resources in Nigeria, from individual and corporate taxes, from oil companies in

Nigeria, owing Nigeria billion of dollars or some trillions of dollars from pollutions to Nigerian lands, and to all Nigerians or their health for the past fifty years. Please see the New York Times of June 16, 2010, and also read the facts in my books *Chevron & Ethics, Vols. 1-4.* Billions of dollars will also come available from curtailing wastes and corruption, drastically reducing government size, and using technology to save billions of dollars, and from money stolen by corrupt Nigerians in Swiss banks and in foreign banks, which according to some estimates are in the billions of dollars! I also intend to generate billions from taxes of wealthy individuals and from criminal prosecution of foreign oil companies polluting Nigeria, etc. Other sources of income will be explained in detail later in this paper. I did so many projects (or was part of so many projects) successfully that were bigger than this one while in the USA army, under budget, without incurring any debt, and with surplus money left every time. Experience counts here, trust me! Nigeria will never again borrow any money from the IMF or World Bank, or any foreign bank, all of which are agents of colonialism and imperialism, and one of the main reasons Nigeria is backward.

3. Every student in the Universities (plus Secondary School students who wish to enter the University early, and that is highly recommended) will be eligible to receive $100-$500 stipends (free money) every month to support themselves while in school.

4. There will be registers in class, where you register your presence in class with your fingerprint in a computer, or hand-signature, since your fingerprint is unique only to you. <u>There will be no room for cheating, since there will be surveillance cameras everywhere in all schools in this new Nigeria</u>. Every Nigerian child and youth is qualified to be enrolled in any university in Nigeria

of his/her choice, even while they are still in Secondary School, without any discrimination. Joint Admission and Matriculation Board or JAMB will be scrapped for good. Admissions will be conducted on the spot, year round, by the university, on a daily basis, except on public holidays, and any student, regardless of his/her age, who can pass (and will be coached over and over again, retrained over and over the same day or in few days, with food provided during coaching, until he/she passes the exams) a simple standardized test, like the ones used to enter community colleges in the United States in Mathematics, English, plus any three languages in Nigeria, like Yoruba or Hausa or Ibo or Ijaw or Itsekiri, etc.

5. Teachers' pay will be increased to $1,500 monthly for elementary/Secondary Schools teachers, and from $3,000-$4,500 monthly for University professors in the arts and humanities. Science and Mathematics professors will make between $4,000 and $10,000 monthly. The qualification for teachers and university professors will be the same as in the United States

or in the UK, teachers must be well trained with quality and quantity education, and must be a specialist in their field, like in the United States, and teachers in the new Nigeria must place so much emphasis on the need for ethics and morality (right from wrong, dos and don'ts, and doing what is right legally and morally) in everything in the new Nigeria and make the students live that life to get any good grade, and teachers must teach more than the basics, by teaching university courses in sciences, Mathematics, ethics, logic and morality in elementary and secondary schools, etc.

6. Nigerians are very smart people, naturally. However, every Nigerian educated in Nigerian schools and universities in the past forty years or so,

and/or in any Third World Country, will be required to go back to attend the new systems of education under my leadership and update their certificates and degrees and the contents of what they were taught, to be on the same level or better, with Harvard, Yale, MIT, Oxford & Cambridge, etc. The new government and the new systems of things under my leadership and management will provide free education with free monetary allowance monthly and feeding for the updates, on weekends or during public holidays for those gainfully employed or too busy. My government will find ways to accommodate every Nigerian to get educated properly to compete well on the global stage, no exception, please. Without the updates, your degrees and certificates <u>will not be given full faith and credit</u> by the new government in Nigeria.

7. Every Nigerian graduating from Nigerian colleges or universities will be required to possess a technical skill or some technical skills. You can choose to enter into the university to study anything you wish. That is fine. However, the new government will required you to also

study and pass most relevant courses offered in the universities, in the arts, humanities and <u>almost all science courses</u>, in order to graduate and do not worry, the new professors, this time, well qualified, well paid, and energetic for the job, will coach all students until they master every subject and its content, until the students are proficient in that subject or course, even if it means coaching the students all day and all night. The new government will provide accommodation, feeding and great salaries for all university professors, who in turn will raise the level of quality and quantity of education to the stars and beyond. It is a must in the new Nigeria, and those professors who cannot do this job (for there will be surveillance cameras in all the classrooms and in government offices to monitor everything) will be quickly sent back for more retraining or early retirement.

8. The beauty of this new system of education in Nigeria is that every Nigerian graduating from Nigerian schools will now be required to get a professional degree, besides their choice of studies. Therefore, every Nigerian will

be required by the new government to have a professional degree in Law or in Medicine or in Engineering or in Nursing, Pharmacy, Science and Technology. If you are going into Law, you are required to have a bachelor's degree first in any subject, and if you are going to study Medicine, you are required to have a bachelor's degree in Biology, just like in the United States, etc. It is a new day in

Nigeria: every Nigerian is going to be paid to attend the university to get a professional degree and/or license in Law, Medicine, Engineering, etc. My government is going to prove to the world that Nigerians are more intelligent, more educated, and better suited to manage and lead any organization or nation better than anyone else, and trust me, within four years or less, the United States, UK, and other so-called industrialized nations of the world will no longer require Nigerians to get visa to visit their countries. Trust me. I am going to make that happen. In fact, all Nigerians will be so happy and satisfied with what the new government under my leadership is providing for them at home that there will be no need to travel to the USA or

London or any foreign country in search of a better life that will never materialize, when all the foreign embassies are doing is collecting the visa fees and denying visas to qualified Nigerians, illegally. Thieves! *Ole!*

9. The educational system will be changed immediately to reflect the same quality of education in the United States (Harvard, Yale, and MIT), and in the UK

(Oxford and Cambridge Universities). However, <u>Nigerian universities will be uniform, and the contents of courses will be uniform and better</u>. Every student in Nigerian colleges and universities, under my leadership, in the new Nigeria, will be very busy daily, <u>will have a lot of fun</u>, will learn how to sing, dance, play piano, guitar, and other musical instruments, will learn how to beat the African drum, will take almost all the courses in the university, including English 1 & 2, College Algebra and pass with a "B" grade average or better to graduate, will understand and speak fluently, at least, <u>any five Nigerian languages</u>, will take German Language, French, Spanish and one another foreign language, will take Chinese language and/or <u>write proficiently in the</u>

<u>Mandarin</u> before graduation. The world has changed. Nigeria needs to change with the world, and **<u>under my leadership</u> <u>Nigeria is going to be ahead of the game, intellectually</u>**. Every Nigerian must study hard and graduate in five years or less with a bachelor and any one professional degree in Law, Medicine, Engineering or a Ph.D., but every Nigerian, in the New Nigeria will

be sponsored with Nigerian money, to become a well skilled, qualified, well educated, professional, no exception, please. Nigerians will be the best in science and technology, the best managers and leaders of Nigerian corporations, of American, European and Chinese corporations outsourcing into Nigeria. Posterity will vindicate me here.

10. Upon graduation from the new educational system, in the new Nigeria, every Nigerian will be given about three million Naira to start a new life. The condition attached is for the graduates with professional degrees in the new Nigeria to commit to work in Nigeria and help the Nigerian government and corporations in Nigeria to grow productively for at least twenty years

after graduation. If not, then the money becomes a loan that must be repaid back to Nigerian government with interests, because that money and free education must be invested in Nigeria, and in Nigeria alone. It will be a crime, or a felony to get this education and free money and travel overseas to live, resulting in brain-drain to Nigeria, no more please. **Together, we must invest in Nigeria**, please.

11. Every college and University in the new Nigeria will have a big farm that produces only organic food (without using pesticides to damage our ecology and our environment), a state-of-the-art science laboratory for Research and Development (or R&D), a teaching hospital well equipped like any one in

the United States and manufacturing plant or plants attached to it, because courses and everything being taught to students in the new Nigeria schools/universities must have real life applications for the students, simultaneously. Every item used for cooking students' meals, notebooks, utensils, in fact, every necessary item needed to function daily will come from the university's agricultural department and/or from the manufacturing plant attached to the university, <u>to be run and managed by students and their professors</u>. Before graduation, every student in Nigerian schools are required to work in the farm, in the science laboratory and in the manufacturing plant attached to every school and gain valuable experiences (at least twelve months of working experience) as part of the professional degrees to be awarded upon graduation.

12. Every car or vehicle used in the new Nigeria will be manufactured in Nigeria. Every engineering department in Nigerian schools will be challenged and funded to manufacture their green cars, using little or no crude oil, preferably, getting 100% of its energy from

renewable energy sources, using solar energy, etc. There will be competitions for the best innovations in the sciences and technology by Nigerian schools monthly and yearly, with millions of dollars awarded to the best science students and professors. Renewable energy from natural resources such as sunlight, wind, rain, tides and biomass will be the order of the new Nigeria for sustainable growth and development.

The new Nigeria under my leadership is going to be a geek, trust me!

13. The new Nigeria will export more quality and quantity products and services, and import almost nothing from China or United States or Europe. In less than four years, my leadership will develop and modernize everything in Nigeria, and be self-sufficient, be the best in

innovation, invest heavily in sciences, technology, and in Nigerian cultures and norms, and move the country to the equals of the G-8 or better!

14. Crime will be almost zero in the new Nigeria because every youth, every Nigerian in College will be paid monthly, will be very productive and busy attending any university, plus study any course of their choice, plus any

professional course, required by the new government.

15. The government will immediately investigates and release all inmates improperly jailed without commission of any crime, <u>empty all jails in Nigeria for the world to see</u>, because a lot of people are unjustly jailed without any commission of a crime, start all over, and prisoners found to have committed

a crime (especially those still sane and whose brains are still intact) will be removed from jail and prison, and be reformed and rehabilitated in a clean environment, provided with the same education in the new system of things, given community service and/or assigned farm work with pay, and part of the prisoners' pay will be given to their victims until they are released, but prisoners will no longer be kept in stinking prisons, but rather in well-kept environment, <u>for everyone deserves humane treatment in the new Nigeria</u>, since there will no longer be need for crime in the first place, and every Nigerian will always be consulted, and all Nigerians will have a say, and their suggestions carefully weighed and followed by my leadership, regarding everything. The <u>Rule of Law</u> will be the new order of the new nation.

16. Police officers and army officers will have the <u>same education, training, duties, responsibilities and salary as their counterparts in the United States</u> and in the UK, etc. Their salaries will start around $1,500 monthly for the lowest rank Police and Army officers and $3,000 to $8,000 monthly for Police

Lieutenant to Inspector-General of Police. Those in the rank of Colonel through General in the Nigerian Army will make between $4,000 to $10,000 monthly, with free housing, free feeding and great benefits for members of their families.

17. Electrical, Civil and Mechanical Engineering departments in Colleges and universities in the new Nigeria will

ensure power or electricity used on our colleges and its neighborhoods is from renewable energy sources by using <u>residential solar panels</u>, <u>biomass power</u> or the recovery of energy from wastes or trash, like in Turkey, and from other renewable energy sources, like renewable energy from <u>natural resources such as sunlight, wind, rain,</u>

tides and others and not from petroleum.

18. Green initiatives and sustainable business practices are number one priority for the new systems of things.

19. Other sources of income for the government for all these goodies in the new Nigeria will also come from taxes from wealthy Nigerian, big corporations and from untapped natural resources,

like gold, natural gas, and <u>so many natural resources in Nigeria that remained untapped hitherto</u>, from the sale of fresh, drinkable water and bottled water, (water being the next equivalent of crude oil) to rich countries like China, Europe, India and USA, and from money to be recovered from foreign nations and individuals who have stolen from Nigeria for several decades. I know these foreign countries and individuals. As an American Soldier, I am the only one well suited to demand for reparation, quietly, from these foreign countries and individuals, who will comply fully, because I have the secret documents and weapons, and am privy to a lot of underground dealings, and theft from Nigeria, worth billions of dollars, before and after independence from Great Britain in 1960. <u>I know what to do and how, with respect, without embarrassing these foreign crooks and individuals, to refund the loots gotten from Nigeria.</u> **But, I am going to be very firm**. With all due respect, there is no other politician in Nigeria right now, except myself, to put that special touch to things, and get billions and trillions of dollars stolen from Nigeria to modernize everything in Nigeria. Please Nigerians: give me the privilege to lead this great nation from the bottom of abyss, to the stars and beyond. I shall not disappoint you. I promise. <u>God willing, together we shall move the new Nigeria forward, progressively, productively, effectively and efficiently.Let us put our house in order, Nigerians. **Together**, we shall win.</u>

20. A New Village and Town will be built by the new government in every State and in the Federal Capital, and this new Village will be well planned, commenced and completed by some of the best engineers in Nigeria, possibly with assistance from the United States Army, Nigerian Army and engineering students and their professors in Nigerian universities. Every power generated or

electricity in these new towns and villages will be from natural sources: sunlight or solar energy, wind power, rain, tides, biomass, etc.

21. <u>Every new professional graduate from the new system of education with professional degree</u> who is a good citizen, working very hard to better the Nigerian society, foreign professionals helping the Nigerian economy <u>and</u>

Nigerians with professional degrees from developed countries (like USA, UK, etc) ready, willing and able to help Nigeria to grow, will be allowed to reside in the apartments and homes built by the new government in these new towns and villages, for rent-to-own system, or the cost to buy a condo (with Certificate of Occupancy) starting at two million naira. Every nook and cranny of these towns and villages will have surveillance cameras (just like every major road and city in the new Nigeria), and living in these towns and villages will be like living in beautiful Colorado or well planned cities in Paris, Florida, etc. The new Nigeria exemplified in these villages and towns will be crime-free, every one residing there will have the very best in education, plus some military training, as part of the new education in the new Nigeria, the new villages and towns will be crime-free, because everyone will have solid skills, and be making enough money, and have great confidence in themselves, and so much respect for themselves and others that there would be no need for crime of any sort anymore. Most important, these new towns and villages will be clean, free of pollution of any kind, because cars driven inside will be powered only by renewable energy, like solar energy. Otherwise, no motorized bikes, only bicycles and two or four wheel peddling devices will be invented and in use in these new towns and villages. The beauty of it and every aspect of these new towns and villages will be unique, creative, and the envy of the world. It will surpass all the best cities in the USA, Europe and Asia, trust me!

22. This is my plan for the new Nigeria. This is the plan I came to the Western World to study for twenty-one years of my life, and now I have all the tools and experiences to make it happen.

23. Again, the money to build and carry the new Nigeria forward, establish new

schools, train and retrain every Nigerian to have marketable skills to compete on a global stage and do better, build and modernize our agricultural systems to surpass the ones in Brazil, build all Nigerian roads and maintain it without giving out any single contract to dubious local and foreign businesses ruining Nigeria, rather, using engineers from the Nigerian Army, university professors and engineering students, with possible assistance from the best engineers in the USA Army, where I am a member, and using the labor of Nigerian prison inmates with pay, after freeing the innocent prisoners, empowering every sector of the Nigerian economy to produce something of the highest quality, and with the cheapest costs ever, to export out to other countries, while producing everything needed in Nigeria by Nigerian universities and by Nigerian corporations, the money for all these projects will be coming from the crude oil and other natural resources in Nigeria, from money owed to Nigeria by the oil companies, which only my candidacy (myself) is clean or only my candidacy has a *clean hand* from the bribes given by the oil companies to

Nigerian politicians, and only my candidacy (myself) is an American Soldier, strong enough to face up to the oil companies and foreign entities and local businesses and individuals who have stolen several trillions of dollars from Nigeria, and I shall have all these funds ready to develop and modernize the New Nigeria without any qualm, and still <u>maintain surplus budget yearly</u> and without borrowing from the IMF or World Bank or those crooks, because I am an American Soldier. I know 'what's up,' ok! In the new Nigeria, every Nigerian, and not just those legislators and people in *Aso Rock* now enjoying the wealth of Nigeria, in the new Nigeria, every Nigerian, man and woman, will have equal access to Nigerian wealth, and all will be treated equally, fairly and justly. Again, the Rule of Law will be the order of the day. All Nigerians will be heard. Human rights will have top priority by the new Nigerian leadership. <u>Human rights violations will be dealt with squarely</u> and **reasonable** <u>remedies</u> will be paid to the victims.

24. There will be <u>technology chief or secretary who reports directly to the</u>

President. Science and technology will have the topmost priority by the new Nigeria. Every child and every student in Nigeria will have a free laptop that does not use electricity, but can be cranked up, to access the internet, to be carried home after school, to do home-work and their work sent to the teachers and professors via the internet before the next class. It is a new dawn Nigerians. Welcome home!

25. **This is my actuality, not a dream, for the New Nigeria**. Now, if I do not get there with you, if I get killed or murdered by the enemies of progress everywhere, please every good Nigeria with good conscience should work hard to make it happen and then pass on the torch to the best of the brightest in Nigeria. I

have the greatest confidence in Nigerians as a people who are naturally very smart and intelligent. But, since the old systems of things in the Nigerian systems could not utilize the brains of Nigerians, it became wasted in crimes, etc. The new government will do the exact opposite and engage all Nigerians and <u>challenge all Nigerians to establish their own businesses and to be creative</u>

and to innovate something creative and unique things to be marketed and sold locally and overseas, and the funds will be provided by the new government under my leadership, through loans, grants, etc. Under the new government, education and retraining, is forever, even after you have graduated with a professional degree from the new system. Again, education, learning, innovation and creativity must be going on forever in the new Nigeria, alright, my brothers and sisters! There will be no time for nonsense. Truth, honesty, hard-work, **integrity**, quality education, logic, will be the order of the day, and he/she who has not worked will not eat, period! No freebies!

26. The plans here for the new Nigeria will have a follow-up, will be modified and

perfected daily, in accordance will suggestions from Nigerians, and new ideas and innovations, etc. But, I am absolutely convinced this is the best way forward for Nigeria, and for all Nigerians. <u>I shall **communicate** with all Nigerians daily and weekly</u>, about the State of our Country, now and into the future. <u>Everything will be **transparent**</u>. I promise. I have the fire burning inside me to make it happen for all Nigerians.

27. As President, I intend to take concrete steps and actions in the first month of being sworn in, to deliver on these promises to make a complete turnaround in Nigeria for the best in education, agriculture, infrastructures, science and technology, **with military discipline and precision**.

BOOKS BY PRINCE GABRIEL AVAILABLE ONLINE OR IN BOOKSTORES WORLDWIDE

1. *Jungle of Confusion*

2. *The Poor Man: The Poor versus The Rich. How to make it from Rags to Riches*

3. *The Complete works of Prince Gabriel*

4. *An American Soldier Protesting Bad Treatment to Women, Children & The Poor*

5. *Funny Stories. Laugh & Laugh*

6. *A cow boy who lost his wife*

7. *Family & Security from Thief*

8. *Safety for Kids: Fun Programs to prevent crimes & make youths productive*

9. *Special Gifts for you*

10. Secrets of Happy Family: Practical things to do to unite & have fun!

11. Sex Me (Ultimate sex techniques)

12. How to be a great leader and a great Manager, both at work & at Home (Part One)

13. How to be a great leader and a great Manager, both at work & at Home (Part Two)

14. How to be a great leader and a great Manager, both at work & at Home (Part Three)

15. How to be a great leader and a great Manager, both at work & at Home (Part Four)

16. How to be a great leader and a great Manager, both at work & at Home (Part Five)

17. How to be a great leader and a great Manager, both at work & at Home (Part Six)

18. How to be a great leader and a great Manager, both at work & at Home (Part Seven)

19. How to be a great Manager and a great Leader, both at work & at Home (Part Eight)

20. How be a great Manager and a great Leader, both at work & at Home (Part Nine)

21. How be a great Manager and a great Leader, both at work & at Home (Part Ten)

22. How be a great Manager and a great Leader, both at work & at Home (Vols. 1-10)

23. Catholic Sex Scandal: Is it time to dissolve the Catholic Church...? Part One

24. Catholic Sex Scandal: Can a woman become a Pope to save the Church? Part two

25. Catholic Church Sex Scandal: Please Forgive the Catholic Church, Part three

26. How to lose weight quickly. Best methods like in the US Army, Part one

27. A Letter from an American Soldier to all poor people in the world: come to America for your survival...come, come, come...

28. When sex and soccer meets. How to score a goal with your lover

29. Raw Meat in Kids Burger at CARL'S JR, Vol. 1

30. PEACE. WORLD PEACE. <u>Specific things to do to have world peace.</u> Part 1, Vol. 1

31. Dog! A Dog is as bad as its owner

32. Chevron is a very good company. Indeed! Vol. 1

33. Chevron & Ethics, Vol. 2

34. Chevron & Ethics Vol. 3

35. Chevron & Ethics, Vol. 4

36. Dating: Dos & Don'ts during Courtship

37. How to Survive this hard time

38. Begging: creative ways

39. Green Initiatives: How to quit Smoking, Vol. 1

40. Conserving Natural Resources & Saving the Earth, Vol. 1

41. My promise to fix everything in Nigeria: My Contract with Nigeria, Vol. 1

42. Libya War is wrong! An American Soldier protesting against the war in Libya, Vol. 1

43. Two books and more: Family & Security from Thieves, Vol. 2, etc.

44. Life in the United States, Asia, Europe & Africa, 1970-2011

45. Libya War, Afghanistan…Please STOP all future wars!

46. Imminent Danger!

47. Pro Life & Pro Choice: you are both right!

48. ANGER Management 1st & 2nd Editions

49. MARRIAGE: How to have a happy & long-lasting marriage

50. INFIDELITY: Legalize it? How to catch a lover/cheater. How NOT to be a cheater/loser like Arnold Schwarzenegger & Tiger Wood (classic book just out!)

Write to me regarding any other business you wish to do with me, like Wealth Management, Partnerships, or any issue, or donations to Breast Cancers or donation to my Charities, etc. Send your letters to:

Prince Gabriel Atsepoyi,   phone: 720 934 1983 USA

Doctorate program

5775 DTC BLVD, SUITE 100

GREENWOOD VILLAGE, COLORADO 80111 USA

OR FAX: 303 694 6673 (USA)

NOTE: BEST WAY TO REACH ME IS VIA EMAIL:

PRINCE.GABRIELL@GMAIL.COM, Gabriel.atsepoyi@yahoo.com

OR

ATSEPOYI@HOTMAIL.COM

An Advice from Prince Gabriel, an American Soldier

Take good care of yourself, eat nutritionally balanced diet, lots of fruits and vegetables, and drink lots of water daily, get at least eight hours of sleep daily (to enable you be in good mood, and show good smile always, and be very productive daily, please), exercise daily, please fall in love have good sex more frequently, keep good friends who are ready to be educated and work hard in life to enjoy their lives, be friendly with everyone regardless of race, gender, ethnicity, creed or religion, make everyone your friend and your family, give to the poor always, help the needy always, reduce waste please, recycle and reduce, plant a tree weekly please, be involved in green initiatives and sustainable business practices, use less air conditioner, generate electricity freely from nature, through solar energy, wind power, and others, be the first to say hello to friends and strangers, be smart and stay away from trouble always, talk less, listen more, better yourself daily, improve your life daily, forgive always, respect and protect girls and women always, laugh daily and be around happy people, do humor, take life easy, enjoy life while it lasts, go out and get the millions of dollars waiting for you, since no one is born to be poor, get education and seek information daily, be rich in morality, do those things that are excellent, and have lots, and lots of fun! Bye!

Intentionally left blank

August 20, 1993

Mr. Gabriel B. Atsepoyi
8826 E. Florida Ave. #101
Denver, CO 80231

Dear Mr. Atsepoyi,

It was such a delight to receive your book Total Happiness. I am grateful. Your kindness and thoughtfulness are appreciated.

Again, thank you for thinking of me.

Best wishes,

Oprah Winfrey

OW:sb

Can you give hope to others? Can you help to make hope realistic? Can you help to make good things to happen in other people's lives? Can you? Could you please try? Please.

<u>Thank you.</u>

Intentionally left blank

THE BOOK OF TOTAL HAPPINESS
by Gabriel B. Atsepoyi (Akpieyi)

Education is the key to learning any subject better, so why should it be any different when it comes to being happy? This is the premise for Gabriel Atsepoyi's *The Book of Total Happiness*, in which the author gives new meaning to the search for happiness and contentment in one's life.

It has been said that psychological maturity is achieved when one gains a secure understanding of the meaning of life and one's place in it. This fascinating volume explores this matter in full detail concerning happiness, marriage, health and physical well being. Regardless of religious or philosophical persuasion, readers will become engrossed in this presentation, which to its credit does not intend to talk down to readers, but instead provides working guidelines in a straightforward and easily understood fashion.

Given the high rate of divorce these days, Mr. Atsepoyi believes that without some form of education concerning marriage, the do's and don't's, the expectations and the compromises, people are destined to continue to allow this shocking statistic to grow. This book's goal, therefore, is to begin that education, to provide understandable paths toward that elusive spiritual habitat, being happy. It's not as easy as it seems, says the author, and most people have to work at it. Yet, it is not totally out of reach, if one can look at life with honest appraisal and work to change those things that hinder one's happiness.

One of the more intriguing aspects of this book is the point that not everyone achieves the same level of happiness, nor has the same avenues available to them in their search for personal happiness. That is fine, says the author, because no two people are exactly the same. Each must find that place that is comfortable for him or her, then work to maintain those good feelings through effort and commitment.

Mr. Atsepoyi's prose is fluid and expressive, and his observations are shrewdly punctuated by a basic wisdom that will appeal to all. But what makes this book be singled out from the many is the significant contribution it makes toward re-educating people of the how and why of being happy. This serves a most practical purpose, first in helping the reader to find paths and guidelines for being happy, the author is also boldly illustrating the power of individual expression, positive thinking, and having a goal to work toward.

Highly recommended for its insight and analyses, *The Book of Total Happiness*, by Gabriel Atsepoyi, is must reading. The author's ideas are lucid and innovative, portraying much wisdom and common sense, and combining all these attributes into one volume enables each reader to further his or her education on perhaps the most important subject matter existing today, the art of being happy.

Section Two of the book focuses on: A-Z about HIV/AIDS and the latest facts on AIDS, protection for kids and family, women's rights (the need to respect and protect women), smoking and its hazards, environmental protection/prevention, how and the need for better education for children, etc., etc.

THE BOOK OF TOTAL HAPPINESS

ABOUT THE AUTHOR

Gabriel Atsepoyi (Akpieyi), twenty-six years old, was born in Africa and presently resides in Colorado.

An avid reader, Mr. Atsepoyi makes it known that the only way he is happy is when he is helping others. His love of God serves his existence well, as he expands upon his belief that one's knowledge is one's power in leading a happy and successful life.

A member of the Optimist Club of Arvada, the author has had many articles published previously on a variety of topics, yet his overriding concerns are for the rate of divorce and its effects toward broken homes, unhappy families, neglected children, uneducated and uncultured children, and crime. He has propounded many solutions in these areas in his latest work, and his hope is that readers will reflect upon those suggestions.

THE BOOK OF TOTAL HAPPINESS
by Gabriel B. Atsepoyi (Akpleyi)

Education is the key to learning any subject better, so why should it be any different when it comes to being happy? This is the premise for Gabriel Atsepoyi's *The Book of Total Happiness*, in which the author gives new meaning to the search for happiness and contentment in one's life.

It has been said that psychological maturity is achieved when one gains a secure understanding of the meaning of life and one's place in it. This fascinating volume explores this matter in full detail concerning happiness, marriage, health and physical well-being. Regardless of religious or philosophical persuasion, readers will become engrossed in this presentation, which to its credit does not intend to talk down to readers, but instead provides working guidelines in a straightforward and easily understood fashion.

Given the high rate of divorce these days, Mr. Atsepoyi believes that without some form of education concerning marriage, the do's and don't's, the expectations and the compromises, people are destined to continue to allow this shocking statistic to grow. This book's goal, therefore, is to begin that education, to provide understandable paths toward that elusive spiritual habitat, being happy. It's not as easy as it seems, says the author, and most people have to work at it. It is not totally out of reach, if one can look at life with honest appraisal and work to change those things that hinder one's happiness.

One of the more intriguing aspects of the book is the point that not everyone achieves the same level of happiness, nor has the same avenues available to them in their search for personal happiness. That is fine, says the author, because no two people are exactly the same. Each must find that place that is comfortable for him or her, then work to maintain those good feelings through effort and commitment.

Mr. Atsepoyi's prose is fluid and expressive, and his observations are shrewdly punctuated by a basic wisdom that will appeal to all. But what makes this book be singled out from the many is the significant contribution it makes toward re-educating people of the how and why of being happy. This serves a most practical purpose, first in helping the reader to find paths and guidelines for being happy, the author is also boldly illustrating the power of individual expression, positive thinking, and having a goal to work toward.

Highly recommended for its insight and analyses, *The Book of Total Happiness*, by Gabriel Atsepoyi, is must reading. The author's ideas are lucid and innovative, portraying much wisdom and common sense, and combining all these attributes into one volume enables each reader to further his or her education on perhaps the most important subject matter existing today, the art of being happy.

Section Two of the book focuses on: A-Z about HIV/AIDS and the latest facts on AIDS, protection for kids and family, women's rights (the need to respect and protect women), smoking and its hazards, environmental protection/prevention, how and the need for better education for children, etc., etc.

THE BOOK OF TOTAL HAPPINESS
ABOUT THE AUTHOR

Gabriel Atsepoyi (Akpleyi), twenty-six years old, was born in Africa and presently resides in Colorado.

An avid reader, Mr. Atsepoyi makes it known that the only way he is happy is when he is helping others. His love of God serves his existence well and expands upon his belief that one's knowledge is one's power in leading a happy and successful life.

A member of the Optimist Club of Arvada, the author has had many articles published previously on a variety of topics, yet his overriding concerns are for the rate of divorce and its effects toward broken homes, unhappy families, neglected children, uneducated and uncultured children, and crime. He has propounded many solutions in these areas in his latest work, and his hope is that readers will reflect upon those suggestions.

ISBN 0-9636951-0-X

Prince Gabriel, Africa

Intentionally left blank

Intentionally left blank

Intentionally left blank

Intentionally left blank

Intentionally left blank

Intentionally left blank

www.ingramcontent.com/pod-product-compliance
Lightning Source LLC
Chambersburg PA
CBHW031814170526
45157CB00001B/52